1 MONTH OF
FREE
READING

at
www.ForgottenBooks.com

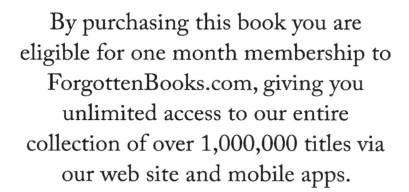

By purchasing this book you are eligible for one month membership to ForgottenBooks.com, giving you unlimited access to our entire collection of over 1,000,000 titles via our web site and mobile apps.

To claim your free month visit:
www.forgottenbooks.com/free177705

ISBN 978-0-265-18271-0
PIBN 10177705

State of Connecticut

PUBLIC DOCUMENT No. 40

THIRD BIENNIAL REPORT

OF THE

ATTORNEY-GENERAL,

FOR THE

Two Years Ended January 3, 1905.

WILLIAM A. KING,

Attorney-General.

Hartford Press:

The Case, Lockwood & Brainard Company,

1905.

TABLE OF CONTENTS.

ACT ESTABLISHING THE OFFICE OF ATTORNEY-GENERAL.

(General Statutes, Revision of 1902.)

CHAPTER 9.

Attorney-General.

§ 145. Election; office; vacancy. There shall be an attorney-general chosen by ballot in the same manner as other state officers on the Tuesday after the first Monday of November, 1902, and quadrennially thereafter, to hold his office for a term of four years from and after the Wednesday following the first Monday of the next succeeding January, and until his successor is duly chosen and qualified. He shall be an elector of this state, and an attorney-at-law of at least ten years' active practice at the bar of this state. His office shall be at the capitol. Any vacancy arising shall be filled by appointment by the governor for the unexpired term.

§ 146. General duties of. The attorney-general shall have general supervision over all legal matters in which the state is an interested party, except those legal matters over which prosecuting officers have direction. He shall appear for the state, the governor, the lieutenant-governor, the secretary, the treasurer, and the comptroller, and for all heads of departments and state boards, commissioners, agents, inspectors, librarian, committees, auditors, chemists, directors, harbor masters, and institutions, and all suits and other proceedings, excepting upon criminal recognizances and bail bonds, in which the state is a party or is interested, or in which the official acts and doings of said officers are called in question in any court or other tribunal, as the duties of his office shall require; and all such suits shall be conducted by him or under his direction. When any measure affecting the state treasury shall be pending before any committee of the general assembly, such committee shall give him reasonable notice of the pendency of such measure, and he shall appear and take such action as he may deem to be for the best interests of the state, and he shall represent the public interest in the protection of any gifts, legacies, or devises intended for public or charitable purposes. All legal services required by such officers and boards in matters relating to their official duties shall be performed by the attorney-general or under his direction. All writs, summonses, or other processes served upon such officer shall, forthwith, be transmitted by them to the attorney-general. All suits or other proceedings by them shall be brought by the attorney-general or under his direction. He shall, when required by either branch of the general assembly, give his opinion upon questions of law submitted to him by either of said branches. He may procure such assistance as he may require. Whenever any petition for divorce shall have been referred to any committee of the general assembly, such committee may give to the attorney-general reasonable notice of all hearings on such petition, and he shall thereupon take such action as he shall deem to be just in the premises, and he shall appear before such committee in such cases whenever in his opinion justice so requires.

§ 147. Biennial reports; bond. There shall be prepared by him and submitted to the governor a biennial report of the doings of his office; and he shall give account to the treasurer of the state for all fees, bills of costs, and moneys received and expended by him by virtue of his office. He shall be duly sworn, and shall give bond in the sum of five thousand dollars.

State of Connecticut.

REPORT OF THE ATTORNEY-GENERAL.

ATTORNEY-GENERAL'S OFFICE,

HARTFORD, JANUARY 3, 1905.

To the Governor of the State of Connecticut:

In compliance with section 147 of the General Statutes I submit my report for the two years ending January 3, 1905.

Matters growing out of the enforcement of the inheritance tax law have demanded much time and attention from this office during the past two years. The estate of Owen B. Arnold of Meriden, inventoried in excess of $250,000, presented the first occasion for litigation. I appealed, in behalf of the State, from an order of the court fixing the inheritance tax, under the following circumstances:

The estate owned stocks and bonds of corporations organized outside of Connecticut, amounting to $75,000, on which the State claimed a tax of three per cent. The Court of Probate refused to allow this claim, and held that as the securities were issued by corporations not organized under Connecticut law they were not subject to the inheritance tax law. The case was taken, by reservation, to the Supreme Court, which tribunal sustained the claim of the State, and ordered the tax paid.

When it is remembered that Connecticut holdings of stocks and bonds of corporations organized outside of the State are very large, the importance of this decision, (Gallup's Appeal, 76 Conn., 617), becomes apparent in its effects on the future revenue which the State should receive from the inheritance tax. Generally, the tax is now being paid to the State in accordance with the law enunciated in that decision. There are, however, two cases now pending in which the estates claim that they are not obliged to pay an inheritance tax on personal property outside of the State, or on money invested in corporations or partnerships organized and existing elsewhere than in Connecticut. One arises in the estate of George F. Gilman, late of Bridgeport, the other in the estate of Mary F. Hopkins, late of Stamford. The valuation of each estate approximates $800,000. The cases are now before our Supreme Court and will come to trial in January, 1905.

The State was compelled to appeal on the same question from the decree of the Court of Probate fixing the inheritance tax due from the estate of Oliver Bulkeley, late of Fairfield, deceased. The demands of the State, however, in that case, were recognized and paid by the executor after the appeal had reached the Superior Court and before trial, and the appeal was withdrawn.

The constitutionality of the law imposing a succession tax was brought before the Supreme Court in Nettleton's Appeal, 76 Conn., 235. The decision, handed down December 18, 1903, sustained the law on every point. Hon. Donald T. Warner was associated with me in the preparation and trial of the case.

The case entitled City of Hartford *vs.* Maslen *et al.*, involving the State's title to the land on which the Capitol stands and land adjacent thereto, was commenced by Attorney-General Phelps shortly before his term of office expired. He continued in the case, had sole charge of it, and acted alone as counsel for the State in the long trial in the Superior Court, and later in the Supreme Court, obtaining a decision in favor of the State before each tribunal. The case is reported in the 76 Conn., 599. This decision sets at rest all questions as to the ownership and control of the Capitol grounds.

Litigation is pending between the State and the City of Norwich over money arising from fines claimed by the State. The constitutionality of the Act creating the State Police is involved among other questions.

Shortly after the recent election of State officers, Mr. Henry T. Blake of New Haven brought proceedings before

Hon. George W. Wheeler, a judge of the Superior Court, claiming that a ballot, cast by Mr. Blake, in a New Haven voting district, had been illegally rejected by the moderator. The ballot was written, and had on it marks admittedly for purposes of identification. The avowed purpose of the proceedings brought before Judge Wheeler was to test the constitutionality of the secret ballot law. The Attorney-General was cited to appear, and, at the suggestion of Judge Wheeler, entered an appearance for the State. The case is still pending on an appeal taken by Mr. Blake to the Supreme Court.

The case as it appeared before Judge Wheeler presented the question of the constitutional right of the elector to cast a written ballot, in defiance of the statute providing that all ballots shall be printed. This claimed right is based on Article Six of our Constitution, which provides that " in all elections of officers of the State, or members of the General Assembly, the votes of the electors shall be by ballot, *either written or printed.*"

In effect, the claim is that this article of the Constitution confers on the elector the right to use either a written or printed ballot, as he may choose, and that the legislature has no power to deprive him of this choice, — as is clearly attempted by the provisions of the secret ballot law, in declaring that all ballots shall be printed.

The recent constitutional convention evidently did not so construe the existing constitution, for it adopted the same language, — " by ballot, either written or printed," and added the words, " or by voting machine authorized by law." . . .

In view of the fact also that since 1889 there has existed a statute declaring that all ballots shall be printed, it is clear that the constitutional convention could not have attached the meaning to the words quoted from Article Six, which Judge Wheeler, while rejecting the Blake ballot on other grounds, held to be the true meaning.

The language used by the constitutional convention in the draft submitted to the people is substantially that of one of the amendments to the constitution pending before the incoming General Assembly. The question is more than liable to arise, whether an amendment framed in that language, authorizing the use of the voting machine, does not leave vested in the elector the constitutional right to use a ballot, written or printed, at his option, even if the General Assembly, after the adoption of the proposed amendment, should declare that all State elections should be conducted by means of voting machines.

During the past year this office has collected from the United States government the sum of $37,821.50, due the State on account of expenses incurred during the late Spanish war. The difficulties attending the collection of these claims were greatly enhanced by the lapse of time since indemnification was authorized by law. Practically, this undertaking resolves itself into establishing, before the department at Washington, the number and value of the various articles of equipment, etc., for which the State claims reimbursement. It involves a mass of details difficult to accurately marshal together after the expiration of five or six years since the Spanish war. Andrew F. Gates, Esq., of Hartford, assisted me in prosecuting the claims. I received much aid from Adjutant-General Cole and Assistant Quartermaster-General Henry C. Morgan. We succeeded in securing a reversal of some former rulings, by which claims amounting to about $1,600, which had been previously rejected, were allowed and paid to the State.

In my opinion there is still equitably due the State from the United States, on account of the Spanish war, not less than $25,000, although, under the rulings of the War Department, it may require additional legislation by Congress before the claims can be effectively recognized.

The negotiations entered into between the States of Connecticut and New York, looking towards ultimate reciprocal legislation in regard to fisheries in Long Island Sound, have resulted in securing from all molestation those of our citizens who are engaged in lobster fisheries in waters within the jurisdiction of New York.

To enable our fishermen to profitably conduct their business in New York waters they must be assured, months in advance of the fishing season, that they will not be arrested by New York officers for alleged violations of the fishery law of New York relating to non-residents. This assurance has been accorded them during the past two years, and is given them for the coming season. Permanent immunity can come, of course, only from legislation.

While it is undeniable that Connecticut has certainly as large interests to be benefited by such reciprocal legislation as has New York, it is apparent that New York is willing to enact legislation fully as concessive as would be sought from Connecticut.

I have had frequent occasion to advise with the Comptroller, in relation to what are known as " State paupers,"— persons who, during the first six months of residence in Connecticut, become a charge on the State. Omitting from consideration those who were the temporary victims of misfortune, there would remain a large number of those called to my attention who had reached the condition of permanent pauperism when they came, or were sent, into Connecticut; and of these a strikingly large percentage were either insane or mentally deficient to an extent unfitting them to be self-supporting. Some of these unfortunates, who were not proper subjects for permanent support by Connecticut, have been returned to the steamship companies which brought them over, and others to the States to which they belonged. One cannot escape the conviction, however, that Connecticut is being called upon to care for many insane paupers who rightfully belong elsewhere, — a condition that could to some extent be obviated by suitable legislation.

In the so-called "Atwood Suits " I did what I could to protect the defendants from Atwood's demands until the General Assembly convened. The General Assembly has the power to dispose of the suits.

The State became a party to proceedings in the Probate Court for the District of New Haven, in which it was sought to remove the settlement of the estate of Henry B. Plant from Connecticut, where the settlement was begun, to New York. The Probate Court had originally taken jurisdiction of the estate on the ground that Mr. Plant was a resident of New Haven at the time of his death. In an action in the Supreme

Court of New York it was determined that he was a resident of New York at the time of his decease. The validity of the payment of a large inheritance tax to Connecticut seemed dependent on the determination of his residence. An arrangement was entered into between the executors of Mr. Plant's will and the State, by which the former relinquished all claim to the tax which Connecticut had received, and the State thereupon ceased to be a party to the proceedings.

Two or three mortgage foreclosure cases scheduled in the report, have been allowed to remain, pending the result of arrangements between the parties preparatory to adjustment.

All the cases in which the State has been a party, and some of the opinions which I have been requested to give in writing, appear in this report.

WILLIAM A. KING,
Attorney-General.

ACTIONS WITHIN THE STATE.

CHARLES NETTLETON'S APPEAL FROM PROBATE.

On April 3, 1903, the Court of Probate for the District of Meriden passed an order fixing the succession tax due the State of Connecticut on property amounting to $152,192.96.

From this order and decree Charles Nettleton, as executor of the will of said Owen B. Arnold, appealed to the Superior Court for the County of New Haven on the first Tuesday of May, 1903. The case was reserved for the Supreme Court of Errors.

The appellant claimed that the act creating the succession tax violated the fourteenth amendment to the Constitution of the United States, and was null and void. The Supreme Court rendered a decision sustaining the law. The case appears in the 76 Conn., 235.

HENRY H. GALLUP, TREASURER, APPEAL FROM PROBATE.

On the 3d day of April, 1903, the Probate Court for the District of Meriden passed an order that property belonging to the estate of Owen B. Arnold, aggregating $75,832, was not subject to a succession tax to the State of Connecticut, on the ground that it consisted of stocks and bonds of corporations organized outside of Connecticut, and was not, therefore, within the jurisdiction of this State for purposes of the succession tax.

From this order and decree the State appealed to the Superior Court for New Haven County on the first Tuesday of May, 1903. The case was reserved for the Supreme Court. A decision was rendered on the 15th day of April, 1904, reversing the decree of the Court of Probate and directing that the property pay the tax due the State. The case is reported in the 76 Conn., 617.

IN RE WOOLSEY R. HOPKINS' APPEAL FROM PROBATE.

On the 19th day of November, 1903, the Probate Court for the District of Stamford ordered Woolsey R. Hopkins, administrator with the will annexed on the estate of Mary Frances Hopkins, late deceased, of said Stamford, to pay to the State of Connecticut a succession tax on $850,889.50, belonging to said estate.

Said Woolsey R. Hopkins, as such administrator, appealed from said order and decree to the Superior Court for Fairfield County on the first Tuesday of January, 1904. The case has been reserved for the Supreme Court, where it is now pending.

The claim of the administrator is that personal property to the amount of $804,995.06 is exempt from the inheritance tax, because it was not physically located within the State of Connecticut. The claim of the State is that all said property is subject to the tax.

The case is on the docket for trial at the term to be holden the third Tuesday of January, 1905.

HENRY H. GALLUP, TREASURER, APPEAL FROM PROBATE.

On the 28th day of December, 1903, the Court of Probate for the District of Fairfield passed an order and decree fixing the succession tax due the State of Connecticut from the estate of Oliver Bulkeley, late deceased, of said Fairfield. Said order and decree directed that said tax be computed on property within the State of Connecticut, and excluded from said computation all personal property outside the State of Connecticut. The property so excluded from paying the succession tax amounted to $64,417.65.

An appeal was taken by the State from said order, so excluding said property, to the Superior Court for the County of Fairfield, on the first Tuesday of March, A.D. 1904.

Before the action came to trial the Supreme Court rendered a decision in Gallup's Appeal covering the points at issue in this case. The case was thereupon settled by the payment of the succession tax to the State on the property excluded. The appeal was withdrawn.

THE STATE vs. HENRY W. TIBBITS, CLERK OF THE CITY COURT OF NORWICH.

This is an action brought to the Court of Common Pleas for New London County, asking that mandamus issue to compel the payment to the State of one-half the amount of fines collected by the City Court of Norwich in certain liquor prosecutions in which the State police furnished evidence.

The defense is based on the provisions of the charter of the city of Norwich, directing the clerk of the City Court to pay fines to the treasurer of the city, and on the further claim that the act of the legislature creating the State police is unconstitutional and void. The complaint is dated August 25, 1904.

The case is pending.

BRIDGEPORT TRUST COMPANY'S APPEAL FROM PROBATE.

George F. Gilman, a resident of Bridgeport, Connecticut, died March 3, 1901. He left a large estate, of which personal property amounting to $706,507.37 was not physically within the State of Connecticut, but was largely situated within the State of New York.

On March 19, 1901, The Bridgeport Trust Company was appointed administrator on his estate by the Probate Court for the District of Bridgeport.

On May 24, 1901, the said administrator returned an inventory showing personal estate of the value of $30,961.17, and on June 17, 1901, returned another inventory showing real estate belonging to said decedent of the value of $106,000. Subsequently this valuation was increased by $3,500, thus making the entire estate in Connecticut, as inventoried, $140,-461.71.

Administration had been meanwhile taken out in New York. The State claimed that all the personal property outside the State of Connecticut should be inventoried by the Connecticut administrator, for the purpose, among others, of computing the tax due to the State.

On the 15th day of June, 1904, the State made application to the Probate Court for the District of Bridgeport, asking the court to order the administrator to inventory all the personal property, including said $706,507.37 located elsewhere than in Connecticut.

Said court, on the 1st day of October, 1904, granted said application, and ordered all said personal property outside the State to be included in the inventory.

From this order The Bridgeport Trust Company, as administrator, appealed to the Superior Court for Fairfield County on the first Tuesday of November, 1904. The case was reserved for the Supreme Court.

The administrator claims that all the personal property outside the State is exempt from taxation, and that, in the event that it is taxable, the State of Connecticut should have objected to the inventories filed, and made application for additional inventories and appraisals, within four months from the date that administration was granted, viz., March 19, 1901, and that by failing to act within said four months the State is barred from action at any future date.

The State contests both these claims.

IN RE APPLICATION OF HENRY T. BLAKE, OF NEW HAVEN, CLAIMING A MISCOUNT OF THE BALLOTS AT THE RECENT ELECTION OF STATE OFFICERS IN NEW HAVEN, ON THE 8TH DAY OF NOVEMBER, 1904.

The application was dated the 9th day of November, 1904, addressed to Hon. George W. Wheeler, a judge of the Superior Court, setting forth the facts on which it was claimed that a ballot, cast by said Henry T. Blake, had been rejected.

Judge Wheeler caused a summons to issue, citing the Attorney-General to appear on the 14th day of November, 1904. The Attorney-General, at the suggestion of the court, entered an appearance for the State.

The matter was subsequently heard by the court, and it was held that the ballot was legally rejected. An appeal from said decision was taken to the Supreme Court in and for the Third Judicial District on the third Tuesday of January, 1905.

ACTIONS WITHIN THE STATE IN BEHALF OF THE SCHOOL FUND.

STATE

v.

EVERETT E. LORD ET AL.

FORECLOSURE OF MORTGAGE.

Brought to the Superior Court for Middlesex County by complaint dated February 16, 1903, and returnable on the first Tuesday of March, 1903.

Arrearages adjusted and suit withdrawn.

STATE

v.

MICHAEL GEARY ET AL.

FORECLOSURE OF MORTGAGE.

Brought to the Superior Court for Hartford County by complaint dated February 16, 1903, and returnable on the first Tuesday of March, 1903.

Title passed to the State July 3, 1903.

STATE

v.

THOS. DENNIS ET AL.

FORECLOSURE OF MORTGAGE.

Brought to the Superior Court for Hartford County by complaint dated February 16, 1903, and returnable on the first Tuesday of March, 1903.

Arrearages adjusted and suit withdrawn.

STATE

v.

LUTHER AND WILLIAM L. GRIFFIN ET AL.

FORECLOSURE OF MORTGAGE.

Brought to the Superior Court for Hartford County by complaint dated December 14, 1903, and returnable on the first Tuesday of January, 1904.

Title passed to the State May 21, 1904.

STATE

v.

MORGAN M. MILLER ET AL.

FORECLOSURE OF MORTGAGE.

Brought to the Court of Common Pleas for Hartford County February 16, 1904, and returnable on the first Tuesday of March, 1904.

Arrearages adjusted and suit withdrawn.

STATE

v.

SAMUEL BENJAMIN ET AL.

FORECLOSURE OF MORTGAGE.

Brought to the Superior Court for Hartford County by complaint dated February 16, 1904, and returnable on the first Tuesday of March, 1904.

Case pending.

STATE

v.

WILBUR E. GOODWIN ET AL.

FORECLOSURE OF MORTGAGE.

Brought to the Superior Court for Hartford County by complaint dated February 16, 1904, and returnable on the first Tuesday of March, 1904.

Title passed to the State July 24, 1904.

STATE

v.

FRANK BRAINARD ET AL.

FORECLOSURE OF MORTGAGE.

Brought to the Superior Court for Middlesex County by complaint dated February 16, 1904, and returnable on the first Tuesday of March, 1904.

Case pending.

STATE

v.

SAMUEL BENJAMIN AND LEWIS WADHAMS ET AL.

FORECLOSURE OF MORTGAGE.

Brought to the Superior Court for Hartford County by complaint dated February 16, 1904, and returnable on the first Tuesday of March, 1904.

Arrearages adjusted and suit withdrawn.

STATE

v.

JOHN E. AND EMMA F. SEIBERT.

FORECLOSURE OF MORTGAGE.

Brought to the Superior Court for Hartford County by complaint dated November 23, 1904, and returnable on the first Tuesday of December, 1904.

Arrearages adjusted and suit withdrawn.

STATE

v.

FRANCIS DONAHUE.

FORECLOSURE OF MORTGAGE.

Brought to the Superior Court for Hartford County by complaint dated November 23, 1904, and returnable on the first Tuesday of January, 1905.

Case pending.

2

AUTHORIZED ACTIONS OUTSIDE THE STATE IN BEHALF OF THE SCHOOL FUND.

STATE *vs.* CHAS. H. SQUIRES *et al.* (#10169).
  Foreclosure of mortgage. Authorized April 20, 1903.
  Attorney, John C. Munger, Toledo, O. Fee for service, $35.
  Title passed to the State Aug. 31, 1903.

STATE *vs.* GEORGE A. LONG. (## 10429-10470.)
  Authorized April 24, 1903.
  Attorney, Wm. H. Phipps, Paulding, O. Fee for services, $25.
  Title passed to the State Dec. 19, 1903.

STATE *vs.* HELEN H. LITTLE. (# 10413.)
  Authorized June 15, 1903.
  Attorneys, Cable & Parmenter, Lima, O.
  Claim adjusted without expense to State.

STATE *vs.* C. D. AND A. E. CHAPMAN. (# 9977.)
  Authorized November 23, 1903.
  Attorney, W. H. Phipps, Paulding, O. Fee for services, $30.
  Property sold at Sheriff's sale and claim of State paid in full.

STATE *vs.* JOS. MORRIS. (# 10363.)
  Authorized December 10, 1903.
  Attorneys, Cable & Parmenter, Lima, O. Fee for services, $25.
  Property sold and State's claim paid in full February 25, 1904.

STATE *vs.* JAMES AND LILLIE I. CLARK. (# 10213.)
Authorized April 2, 1904.
Attorney, John C. Munger, Toledo, O.
Property sold at Sheriff's sale and claim of State paid
in full.

STATE *vs.* J. C. H. ELDER. (# 10400.)
Authorized April 29, 1904.
Attorneys, Sutphen & Sutphen, Lima, O.
Case still pending.

STATE *vs.* CARL H. A. BECKMAN. (# 10734.)
Authorized April 29, 1904.
Attorney, John C. Munger, Toledo, O.
Claim adjusted without expense to State.

STATE *vs.* WM. AND DEBORAH BAKER. (# 10825.)
Authorized August 31, 1904.
Attorneys, Cable & Parmenter, Lima, O.   Fee for serv-
ices, $25.
Property sold and claim of State paid in full, October
12, 1904.

STATE *vs.* ARTHUR E. LECKLIDER. (# 10119.)
Authorized September 26, 1904.
Holbrook & Monsarratt, Attorneys.   Fee for services,
$30.
Claim of State adjusted in full, December 3, 1904.

STATE *vs.* SAML. C. BURKLEY *et al.* (## 10095, 10149, 10202,
10203.)
Authorized September 26, 1904.
Action in foreclosure, probate proceedings.
Attorneys, Holbrook & Monsarrat, Toledo, O.
Case pending.

STATE *vs.* MARGARET TAYLOR *et al.* (# 10078.)
Authorized September 26, 1904.
Attorneys, Holbrook & Monsarrat; residence, Toledo,
O.
Action still pending.

STATE *vs.* JOHN C. BARBER.   (## 9941-9958.)
    Authorized October 26, 1904.
    Attorney, Wm. H. Phipps, Paulding, O.
    Action still pending.

OPINIONS.

In re the powers and duties of the Governor in assisting civil authorities in the suppression of riot and civil commotion.

HARTFORD, February 5, 1903.

To HIS EXCELLENCY, THE GOVERNOR:

You ask me to define in writing your duties and powers under section 2992 of the General Statutes. I submit the following as my opinion of the limits of those duties and powers.

If riot or civil commotion prevail in a place, and the civil authority is not able to preserve the peace, then, on information, as prescribed in section 2992, it would be within your powers to order out such portion of the National Guard as you might think proper to assist the civil authorities in preserving the peace.

It is not your legal duty to order out the National Guard for this purpose unless you are satisfied that the civil authorities are unable to keep the peace.

The National Guard can not be substituted for the civil authorities to keep the peace, but is to be used solely for the purpose of assisting the civil authorities, and then only when the latter absolutely and imperatively need such assistance.

In the event that the civil authorities of a place, by themselves, and with such assistance as they are empowered to summon and are able to secure, are unable to suppress riot or civil commotion, then it would be within your legal power to assist the civil authorities to keep the peace in the manner prescribed by the statute; and this would be true whether the insufficiency of the civil authorities arises from inadequacy in force or from any other reason.

When the National Guard has been ordered to a place for the purposes set forth in the statute it is not within your legal power to retain the National Guard at that place after the civil authorities are able to reasonably keep the peace. In other words, it is not your duty to allow the National Guard to remain at a place for the sole purpose of guarding property which may be threatened with attack, nor for the sole purpose of meeting an emergency which may arise in the future.

Occasional disturbances, although not altogether slight in their nature, which the civil authorities with all the civil assistance at their command may well be assumed capable of successfully contending with, do not constitute the condition of " riot or civil commotion " which the statute contemplates as warranting the assistance of the National Guard.

The constitution makes the military subordinate to the civil authority, and the National Guard can not be used to take the place of the civil authority; it may be used to assist the civil authorities, but then only when you are satisfied that the civil authority is unable to keep the peace within the meaning of the statute.

I am very respectfully,

WILLIAM A. KING,
Attorney-General.

LIFE INSURANCE POLICY.

Meaning of phrase "A new policy shall be issued for the whole amount of even dollars of annual premiums received by the company.

HARTFORD, February 19, 1903.

HON. THERON UPSON, Insurance Commissioner, Hartford, Conn.

My Dear Sir: — You ask my construction of the following clause in a life insurance policy:

"And the said company does further promise and agree that if after having received not less than three (3) annual premiums this policy shall be surrendered while in force, a new policy shall be issued for the whole amount of even dollars of annual premiums received by the said company (subject to any indebtedness on account of premiums), without subjecting the assured to any subsequent charge except the interest annually in advance on all indebtedness on this policy."

In my opinion the phrase in the above clause "a new policy shall be issued for the whole amount of even dollars for annual premiums received by the said company" would be construed to mean the net amount of money paid by the policy-holder, *i. e.,* the total amount of annual premiums, less the dividends received from the company by the policy-holder. In no event, I think, would the courts hold that the new policy should exceed in amount the face value for which the old policy was written.

I reach this conclusion, not because the language used is not naturally susceptible of another interpretation, but because the courts in similar cases adopt this construction.

I am very respectfully,

WILLIAM A. KING,

Attorney-General.

BOARD OF PAROLE.

Defining the powers of the Board of Parole in relation to prisoners detained in state prison for non-payment of fines.

HARTFORD, February 20, 1903.

To HON. ALBERT GARVIN AND HON. THOMAS D. WELLS, Committee of the Board of Parole.

Gentlemen: — I have before me your communication, reading as follows:

WETHERSFIELD, CONN., Feb. 17, 1903.

HON. WILLIAM A. KING,

Attorney-General,

Hartford, Conn.

DEAR SIR : —

A convict committed to the state prison on Jan. 7, 1902, for not less than one year or more than two years was also sentenced to pay a fine of $100, which, in default of payment, will have to be worked out in prison. Under section 2914 of the General Statutes a prisoner held for non-payment of fine is allowed $100 per year for his labor.

Will you kindly advise us whether prospective detention in prison for non-payment of fine renders ineligible for parole a convict who is otherwise qualified for conditional release? And is a prisoner while working out a fine entitled to earn any deduction of his sentence for good behavior?

Very truly yours,

ALBERT GARVIN,
THOMAS D. WELLS,
Committee of Board of Parole.

The answer to your first question is determined by section 1536 of the General Statutes, which section I quote:

"Any person sentenced to the state prison, after having been in confinement within said prison for a period not less than said minimum term, may be allowed to go at large on parole in the discretion of a majority of the board of directors of said prison and the warden thereof, acting as a board of parole, if in their judgment said prisoner will lead an orderly life if set at liberty."

This section empowers the board of parole to act on the expiration of the minimum term of imprisonment, and a parole may then be granted for the maximum term, whether that maximum term consists of a sentence for years, or of such sentence for years plus imprisonment for non-payment of a fine.

Section 1540 authorizes the board of parole, under the limitations therein stated, to absolutely discharge a prisoner during the period of parole. This section would be inconsistent with a construction of section 1536 other than that above given, and removes, I think, all doubt as to your powers under section 1536.

To your second question I reply that a prisoner in state prison working out a fine is entitled to earn a deduction from his sentence by good behavior.

Section 2914 reads as follows:

"Every prisoner held in said prison for non-payment of a fine shall be allowed one hundred dollars a year for his labor, from the time when his imprisonment for non-payment of said fine commenced, if, in the opinion of the warden and directors, he shall have been submissive to the officers of the prison during his confinement, and conducted himself as a faithful prisoner."

The sentence to pay a fine of one hundred dollars, as in the case instanced by you, is in effect a sentence to imprisonment for one year unless the fine is paid. The prisoner has the option to pay the fine in money or in labor as a prisoner. If not paid in money, each one hundred dollars of fine may be paid by one year of imprisonment, or, as the statute phrases it, the prisoner "shall be allowed one hundred dollars a year for his labor." If because of non-payment of a fine imprisonment results, then, in my opinion, section 2900 of the General Statutes applies, and the prisoner is entitled to commutation for good behavior.

I am very respectfully,
WILLIAM A. KING,
Attorney-General.

FRANCHISE FEES.

Preliminary franchise fee in cases of applications to the General Assembly for special charters. Meaning of the term "private interests" used in Section 10 of the General Statutes in relation to special legislation.

HARTFORD, February 24, 1903.

To HONORABLE HENRY H. GALLUP, Treasurer of the State, Hartford, Conn.

My Dear Sir: — I have before me your communication, in which you request advice as to what class of corporations should pay the preliminary fee of one hundred dollars, pursuant to section 10 of the General Statutes.

That portion of the section relating to this matter reads as follows:

"No application for any act or resolution of incorporation for any commercial or manufacturing corporation, or for any corporation without capital stock, shall be heard by the General Assembly or any committee thereof unless the applicants shall have first paid to the state treasurer a fee of one hundred dollars."

The object of this statute was to subject to the payment of a fee those commercial or manufacturing corporations, and corporations without capital stock, for the formation of which provision had been made by the general law of the State. In my opinion the language of the statute expresses that intent. I therefore advise you that the fee of one hundred dollars is chargeable on every application to the General Assembly for a charter for a commercial or manufacturing corporation, or for a corporation without capital stock, when the general purpose and object for which the charter is sought might have been obtained by organizing under existing corporation laws.

You also ask advice relative to the meaning of the remaining part of the statute, and whether it includes municipal corporations in the class chargeable with the printing fee of five dollars per page. I quote that portion of Section 10 which applies to this matter.

" Upon every bill or resolution affecting private interests, other than appropriation bills or resolutions, passed by the General Assembly, there shall be paid for the use of the State a fee of five dollars for each legal page or fractional part thereof."

The decision of your question really turns on what the legislature meant to include in the term " private interests." There are certain governmental duties incumbent on municipal corporations to perform, in the performance of which they can hardly be considered other than as instruments of the State. On this point the court, in United States vs. B. & O. R. R. Co., 17 Wallace, 322, says :

" A municipal corporation is a representative not only of the·State, but is a portion of its governmental power. It is one of its creatures, made for a specific purpose, to exercise within a limited sphere the powers of the State."

In my opinion bills or resolutions relating to these governmental duties would not come within the meaning of the phrase " private interests " used in the statute. The test by which to determine whether a duty is governmental or not is not altogether uniform. The Supreme Court, in Judd *et al. vs.* Hartford, 72 Conn., 353, holds that "municipal duties are governmental when they are imposed by the State for the benefit of the general public. They may sometimes have that character, also, when imposed in pursuance of a general policy, manifested by legislation affecting similar corporations, for the particular advantage of the inhabitants of the municipality, and only through this, and indirectly, for the benefit of the people at large."

Chief Justice Butler, in Jewett *vs.* New Haven, 38 Conn., 389, lays down the test as follows:

" There is no mode by which to determine whether a power or duty is governmental or not except to inquire whether it is in its nature such as all well-ordered governments exercise generally for the good of all, and one whose exercise all citizens have a right to require, directly or by municipal agency, and whether it has ever been assumed or imposed, as such, by the government of this State, and would have been exercised by the State if it had not been by the city."

Under the provisions of the statute, strictly construed on the lines above suggested, bills or resolutions affecting municipalities in their governmental functions would not be included within the term " affecting private interests," while bills or resolutions relating to municipalities otherwise than in their governmental duties might be included within the term. In my opinion the legislature did not intend to give a meaning to this statute which would require differentiation to the extent that must follow if the statute is to be thus construed. I think it was intended to either wholly exclude or wholly include municipal corporations by the term " private interests." The words do not wholly include the interests of municipal corporations. I am led, therefore, to the conclusion that municipal corporations were not intended to be included in the class which is subject to the tax of five dollars per page. I therefore advise you that all bills or resolutions relating to municipal corporations are excluded from the operation of this portion of the statute.

This, I understand, has been the practice, which has been

followed for some years, and, indeed, ever since the statute was enacted.

I am very respectfully,

WILLIAM A. KING,
Attorney-General.

TAXATION OF SHARES OF STOCK OWNED BY RELIGIOUS CORPORATIONS.

Section 2331 of the General Statutes making it the duty of certain corporations to pay a tax on its capital stock includes in such payment shares of stock owned by religious, charitable, and educational associations.

HARTFORD, February 24, 1903.

HON. HENRY H. GALLUP, Treasurer, Hartford, Conn.

My Dear Sir: — I am in receipt of the following communication:

TREASURY DEPARTMENT,
HARTFORD, February 20, 1903.

HON. WILLIAM A. KING,
Attorney-General.

SIR: —

Section 2331 of the General Statutes makes it the duty of certain corporations to pay a tax on each share of its stock. Does this include each share of stock owned by religious, charitable, and educational associations, whose property is exempt from taxation by Sections 2317, 2318, or by special charter?

Very respectfully,

HENRY H. GALLUP,
Treasurer.

I quote the sections referred to, or so much thereof as is material to the question you place before me:

" SECTION 2331. The secretary, treasurer, or cashier, of every bank, national banking association, trust, insurance, investment, and bridge company, whose stock is not exempt from taxation, shall annually in October, on or before the fifteenth day thereof, file in the office of the tax commissioner of this State a statement under oath, showing the number of shares of its capital stock and the market value thereof on the first day of October, the name and residence of each stockholder, and the number of shares owned by each on said last-named date, and on or before the last day of the following February each of the corporations aforesaid shall collect from its stockholders and pay to the treasurer of this State a tax of one per cent. on the market value of each share of its stock, as such value may be determined under the provisions of section 2332, less the amount of taxes paid by such corporation upon its real estate in Connecticut during the year ending on the first day of said February, all of which real estate shall be assessed and taxed in the town or other taxing district within which it is located.   Every such corporation shall have a lien upon the shares of its stockholders, respectively, for the payment of such taxes."

"SEC. 2317.   The funds and estate which have been or may be granted, provided by the State, or given by any person or persons to the president and fellows of Yale University, the board of trustees of the Sheffield Scientific School, Trinity College, or Wesleyan University, and by them respectively invested and held for the use of such institutions, shall, with the income thereof, remain exempt from taxation; *provided, however,* that neither of said corporations shall ever hold in this State real estate free from taxation affording an annual income of more than six thousand dollars.

"SEC. 2318.   Any church or ecclesiastical society in this State may have and hold exempt from taxation personal property consisting of bonds, mortgages, or funds invested, to an amount not exceeding in value the sum of ten thousand dollars; *provided* that such personal property shall be held solely for the uses of such society, and the revenue derived therefrom shall be used exclusively for the maintenance of public worship and the ordinary expenses incident thereto; and *provided* that such society shall not have and hold property exceeding in value twenty thousand dollars in personal or real estate which is exempt from taxation, otherwise than by virtue of the provisions of this section."

I advise you that it is the duty of every corporation embraced in the classes specified in section 2331 to pay to you on or before the last day of February the tax on each share of stock computed as prescribed in that section, with no deduction on account of the exemptions set forth in sections 2317 and 2318.

The law-making power clearly intended that section 2331 should cause a tax to be paid on the entire capital stock of each of the corporations embraced within its provisions, irrespective of the individual ownership of the shares. This was one of the objects, if not indeed the principal object, sought to be attained by the enactment of that section. That it did not contemplate that exemption of this class of property from taxation should be longer enjoyed by the corporations and societies referred to in sections 2317 and 2318 is evident from the language of section 2334, where it is provided that under certain limitations the corporations and societies mentioned in sections 2317 and 2318 shall be entitled to a payment from the treasurer of a sum not exceeding one per cent. upon the market value of the shares of stock held in any of the corporations specified in section 2331. It is not conceivable that this payment would have been authorized unless section 2331 included within its provisions the corporations and societies hitherto exempted by sections 2317 and 2318. Therefore, so far as these last-named sections provided for exemption from taxation of the funds of the corporations and societies referred to therein, I advise you that those exemptions no longer attach to funds which are invested in the stocks of corporations specified in section 2331.

Our Supreme Court, in Yale University vs. New Haven, 71 Conn., 316, defines the policy of the State in the matter of taxation towards the organizations included in sections 2317 and 2318. It may be claimed that the enactment of section 2331 would constitute a decided change in that policy. This may be conceded without in any way minimizing the fact that the State through its legislature has the power to change that policy if it sees fit. The effect of section 2331, however, would seem to be in the nature of a limitation rather than a decided change. Just as section 2317 places a limit on the real estate that may be held exempt from taxation, so section 2331 places a limitation on the class of personal property that may be so held.

Thus far I have considered only exemptions hitherto provided for by sections 2317 and 2318. Your question includes the effect on section 2331 of exemptions provided for in " special charters." It is common knowledge that " special charters " are numerous in Connecticut. Exemptions from taxation to a greater or less extent have been embodied in some of these charters. Since the decision of our Supreme Court in the case Lord *vs.* Litchfield, 36 Conn., 116, the exemption from taxation granted either by a statute or by a " special charter " has not been considered as beyond the reach of legislative repeal, unless the statute or charter constituted in effect a contract.

In my opinion any exemption from taxation given by a " special charter," that is not in effect a contract, would not prevail as against the provisions of section 2331. To determine whether a charter was of that nature would require an examination of its provisions and the circumstances attending its creation. You will thus see the difficulty of giving an absolutely general answer to this part of your communication; a difficulty which would eliminate itself in the case of any particular corporation existing under a " special charter."

Subject to the above reservation, which, because of its remoteness, I consider as not really affecting the situation, I advise you that section 2331, to the extent that funds are invested in the stocks of corporations mentioned therein, revokes exemptions from taxation which are contained in " special charters."

I am very respectfully,

WILLIAM A. KING,

Attorney-General.

LEGISLATIVE APPROPRIATIONS.

The General Assembly in making appropriations to hospitals is not
limited to the amounts prescribed in Section 2852 of the General
Statutes; neither is it bound by the provisions of Section 65 of the
General Statutes relating to the erection of a building by the
State.

HARTFORD, March 25, 1903.

TO THE JOINT STANDING COMMITTEE ON APPROPRIATIONS.

Gentlemen: — You ask me whether section 2852 of the
General Statutes is within the limitations prescribed by section 23. Section 2852 reads as follows:

" Five thousand dollars shall be annually paid from the
state treasury to each of the following institutions, to wit:
the General Hospital Society of Connecticut, the Hartford
Hospital, the Bridgeport Hospital, the Grace Hospital Society of New Haven, the William W. Backus Hospital of
Norwich, the Norwalk Hospital of Norwalk, and the Memo-
rial Hospital of New London, to be expended under the direction of the Governor of the State and the managers of said
institutions, respectively, for the support of charity patients,
and so used as to benefit the different towns as they may
from time to time make application; a report of which ex-
penditure shall be made biennially to the General Assembly;
provided, however, that no part of said appropriation shall
be paid to any of said hospitals, unless the same be in actual
operation."

The following is that part of section 23 which is germane
to your question:

" The committee on appropriations shall carefully inves-
tigate the estimates and other matters submitted to them, and
they shall report from time to time such appropriation bills
as they may deem necessary for carrying on the different departments of the State government, and for providing for
such institutions and persons as are proper subjects for State
aid under existing laws, for two years from the following
thirtieth day of September. The committee on appropriations shall not have power to report, and the General Assembly shall not make, an appropriation by way of salary, com-

pensation, or fees, or allowances for any purpose in excess of the amount allowed by law, to any particular person or purpose, whenever the same is fixed by law, unless the amount of such salary, compensation, fees, or allowances shall be raised by a statute which has gone into effect at the time when the appropriation is made."

In my opinion, section 2852 is included within the limitations prescribed in section 23. In substance section 23 says that no General Assembly shall appropriate more than five thousand dollars to any of the institutions named in section 2852, and that the committee on appropriations shall not have power to report an appropriation in excess of five thousand dollars for any of said hospitals, in the absence of a statute permitting a larger appropriation.

I advise you, however, that the present General Assembly has full power to increase the appropriation beyond the sum of five thousand dollars to any of the institutions named in section 2852 if it sees fit to do so. The present General Assembly in this matter is not bound by sections 23 and 2852. It would have the power to absolutely repeal both of those sections if it saw fit, and there is no doubt whatever that it can increase these appropriations regardless of the existence of the sections in question. If the committee on appropriations report an appropriation for any of the institutions set forth in section 2852 in excess of the amount fixed by that statute, it would, possibly, be a technical violation of the provisions of section 23. If, however, your report was adopted your act in so reporting would be validated. It is unquestioned law that in a matter of this nature one legislature is not bound by the laws enacted by a preceding legislature. Section 23 embodies an attempt to bind succeeding legislatures in matters which are peculiarly within the province of succeeding legislatures to act upon as they see fit. Pursuant to your suggestion I submit an amendment to section 23, which would, if enacted, relieve it from its present apparent inconsistency.

You also request my opinion as to the effect of section 65 in preventing the State erecting a building except in com-

pliance with the provisions of that section.   Section 65 reads
as follows:

"Whenever estimates shall be made for the erection of
any new building, or additions to existing buildings, the person preparing the estimates shall furnish the Treasurer with
plans and specifications of the same.   No appropriation shall
be made for the erection or construction of any building, or
for any wing or addition to the same, in which the State is
to own or control any part, until complete architectural working plans and specifications of such building, wing, or additions have been delivered to the State Treasurer, and not
until the said Treasurer has advertised continuously in one
daily or two weekly newspapers in each county of this State
for at least two weeks for bids or proposals to construct the
same, and not until such plans and specifications, together
with all bids or proposals that have been received by the
Treasurer, have been considered by the appropriation committee.   No bids shall be advertised for by the Treasurer, unless, in the opinion of the Governor, Comptroller, and Treasurer, or a majority of said officers, such building, wing, or
addition is reasonably necessary."

In my opinion, the General Assembly has the power to
vote an appropriation for the erection of a building for the
State without complying with the provisions of section 65.
You will observe that section 65 is simply another attempt
on the part of one legislature to bind a succeeding legislature
concerning a matter in which the succeeding legislature
cannot be bound.   Of course, I do not express an opinion as
to the wisdom of disregarding the provisions of section 65
in the case of the construction of a building belonging to the
State.   I advise you, however, that the General Assembly
has the power to vote an appropriation and order a building
constructed in such way as it shall determine regardless of
the existence of the provisions of section 65.

I am very respectfully,

WILLIAM A. KING,

Attorney-General.

IN THE MATTER OF THE SOUTH NORWALK VETO.

Meaning of the word " days" in Section 12, Article Fourth of the Constitution, limiting the time during which the Governor may exercise the veto power; decisions of courts of last resort of other states on similar language; effect of long continued practice by the executive department, acquiesced in by the legislature, in construing the word to mean legislative days.

HARTFORD, April 21, 1903.

TO THE SENATE:

On April 17, 1903, I received from your Honorable Body Senate Resolution No. 71, of which the following is a copy:

STATE OF CONNECTICUT,
GENERAL ASSEMBLY,
JANUARY SESSION, A.D. 1903.

Resolved by the Senate:

The attorney-general is hereby requested to give his opinion in writing to the Senate, at his earliest convenience, as to whether under the following statement of facts there is now in legal existence a town of South Norwalk in this state.

House Joint Resolution No. 25, providing for the creation of a town to be known as the town of South Norwalk, passed both the House of Representatives and the Senate during the present session of the General Assembly, and being duly engrossed and attested was presented to the Governor on Wednesday, April 1st. Both houses of the General Assembly were in session on April 1st, 2d, 7th, and 8th. Neither house was in session on April 3d, 4th, 5th, or 6th. April 5th was Sunday.

On Wednesday, April 8th, the Governor returned said resolution to the House of Representatives, wherein it originated, with his objections, and on the same day said House proceeded to reconsider said resolution. Said objections were entered on the Journals of said House. After said reconsideration, viz., on Thursday, April 9th, said House determined by vote taken by yeas and nays that said resolution should not be passed.

The questions hereby presented to the attorney-general for his opinion are:

1. Was the action of the Governor in the return of said resolution to the House, as herein related, on April 8th, taken within the time limited in the Constitution?

2. Do the actions of the Governor and of the House of Representatives, taken as herein related, in any way affect the legal force and validity of House Joint Resolution No. 25, passed by both houses of the General Assembly, as herein related?

3. Is House Joint Resolution No. 25, under the facts herein related, now a law of this state?

Section 146 of the General Statutes provides that the Attorney-General " shall, when required by either branch of the General Assembly, give his opinion upon questions of law submitted to him by either of said branches. He may procure such assistance as he may require." In preparing an opinion in response to your resolution I procured the assistance of Hon. Dwight Loomis and Charles E. Gross, Esq., and they have stated to me that they concur in this opinion which I submit to you.

The answer to your three questions depends upon the meaning of Section 12, Article Fourth, of the Constitution of our State. So much of that section as is material to those questions I quote:

" Every bill which shall have passed both houses of the General Assembly shall be presented to the Governor. If he approves, he shall sign it and transmit it to the Secretary, but if not, he shall return it to the house in which it originated, with his objections, which shall be entered on the journals of the house, who shall proceed to reconsider the bill. If the bill shall not be returned by the Governor within three days, Sundays excepted, after it shall have been presented to him, the same shall be a law, in like manner as if he had signed it, unless the General Assembly, by their adjournment, prevents its return, in which case it shall not be a law."

It appears in your statement of facts that the bill in question, which in this case is a house joint resolution, was presented to the Governor on the first day of April. The current of authorities is substantially unvarying to the effect that the day of presentation, viz., the first day of April, must be excluded in the computation of the three days. In other words, the Governor was entitled to three full days beginning at midnight of April 1st in which to return the resolution. The statement of facts further shows that the resolution was returned by the Governor to the House on the 8th of April, and that this was the third day on which the Legislature was in *actual* session after the day of presentation. If the word " days " as used in the Constitution means days on which the Legislature is in *actual* session, then in my opinion the return of the resolution on the 8th day of April was within the time limit fixed and the veto would be of full force and effect.

So the first debatable question seems to be this: Does the Constitution by the word "days" mean days on which the Legislature is in actual session or does it use the word in its natural and ordinary meaning?

Cooley's Constitutional Limitations, page 73, in the chapter entitled "Construction of State Constitutions" lays down this rule: "In interpreting clauses we must presume that words have been employed in their natural and ordinary meaning. As Marshall, C. J., says: The framers of the Constitution and the people who adopted it must be understood to have employed words in their natural sense, and to have intended what they said."

What then is the meaning of "day" in its natural and ordinary sense? Bouvier's dictionary, adopting Blackstone's definition, defines it as the space of time which elapses between two successive midnights. Our Supreme Court, in Miner *vs.* Goodyear Glove-Mfg. Co., 62 Conn., 411, says: "In ordinary speech a day is that space of time in which the earth makes one revolution on its axis. . . . The civil day is from midnight to midnight." Endlich on Statutes, Section 534, says: "A day in common acceptation and ordinarily in a Constitution means a civil day of twenty-four hours, beginning and ending at midnight."

The justices of the Supreme Court of New Hampshire, in construing a section in the Constitution of that State almost identical with the section of our Constitution now under discussion, held that the word "day" meant a "civil day beginning and ending at midnight," and that the term "five days" did not mean five days on which the Legislature was in actual session, but did mean five ordinary, calendar, or civil days. Opinion of the Justices, 45 N. H., 607. On substantially the same question — the meaning of the word "days" in that clause of the Constitution of Illinois providing for a veto by the Governor — the Supreme Court of Illinois held that "days" meant civil days as defined above. The court said: " It was, however, urged that the framers of the Constitution intended legislative and not natural days. . . . It is not so expressed and the language employed seems to be so plain and explicit that I am at a loss to perceive how it will bear construction. The framers of that instrument seem to have used every pre-caution and reasonable effort to avoid obscurity and as far as possible to avoid necessity for construction. This is mani-fested in this very section, where Sundays are in terms ex-cluded, and yet in law they would generally be excluded, as they are not judicial days." . . . People vs. Hatch, 33 Ill., 137.

To the same effect are the decisions of the courts of last resort in other states on this precise meaning of the word day as affecting the time which a Governor may hold a bill.

Corwin vs. Comptroller, 6 S. C., 390.
Beaudeau vs. The City of Cape Girardeau, 71 Mo., 393.
Harpending vs. Haight, 39 Cal., 189.
State vs. Michel, 52 La Ann, 936 (49 L. R. A., 218).
Miller vs. Hurford, 11 Neb., 377.

In view of the above decisions and of the fact that I find no decisions to the contrary, I feel compelled to say that in my opinion the word " days " in Section 12, Article Fourth, of the Constitution means calendar or civil days and not days on which the Legislature is in actual session; and that the three days which the Governor had for the consideration of the reso-lution in question were the three calendar days beginning at midnight of the first of April, and included April 2d, 3d, and 4th.

I understand from your statement of facts that the House adjourned on April 2d until April 7th, and that the Senate voted a like adjournment. The next question is whether this was the adjournment of the General Assembly contemplated by the Constitution as preventing the return of the bill within three days to the house in which it originated. It is common knowledge that each branch of the General Assembly adjourns its own sittings from time to time during the session, but the

General Assembly itself very rarely adjourns except at the close of the session. All the authorities, without any deflection, so far as I have been able to examine them, have held that the term "adjournment" as used in the corresponding section of the Constitutions of other states means the final adjournment of the General Assembly. The New Hampshire case which I have above quoted in deciding this question says:

"The adjournment referred to in this provision of the Constitution is not, we think, the ordinary recess or adjournment from time to time during the continuance of the session, but the final adjournment at the close of the session. In fact this is the only adjournment, we think, which could prevent the return of the bill within the time limited. . . . Now, the bill must be returned to the house in which it originated, and if it should be held that it must be returned to that house while in session, an adjournment of that house over one day would prevent the return of the bill during that day as much as an adjournment of both houses would, and if it had been intended to provide against such an adjournment for a day . . . the constitutional provision should have been that the bill should be returned in five days to the house in which it originated unless that house shall prevent it by an adjournment. But no such provision is made."

To the same effect are the decisions in Harpending vs. Haight, Corwin vs. Comptroller-General, Miller vs. Hurford, and State vs. Michel, which I have cited above. I find no authority in conflict with these decisions.

Upon the question how the bill should be returned when the house in which it originated is not in session on the last day during which the Governor is authorized to hold the bill, the decisions of the courts are somewhat conflicting. In Harpending vs. Haight, referring to the return of the bill by the Governor when the house in which it originated is not in session, the court says: "It" [the return] "must be a step taken by which his own time for deliberation is ended and that for the deliberation of the Senate is begun; that the bill itself must be put beyond the executive possession; that it must be placed into the possession, actual or potential, of the Senate itself."

And the court there held that it was not necessary to return it to the house while in session. The Louisiana case above cited holds " that if the house in which the bill proposed to be vetoed originated should happen not to be in session when the Governor's message arrived, delivery of the bill, with the Governor's objections, to the presiding officer of the body, or to its clerk, would seem, according to the adjudicated cases, to suffice ; and in case neither the presiding officer nor the clerk can be found, its deposit on the presiding officer's table or desk or in the office of the clerk would doubtless likewise suffice."

This is also the doctrine enunciated in New Hampshire and South Carolina in the cases which I have cited from those states. It is also apparently sustained in the Circuit Court of the United States, U. S. vs. Allen, 36 Fed. Rep., 174.

In the People vs. Hatch, 33 Ill., p. 135, the court lays down a different doctrine. It is there held " that unless the body was in session he would be unable to return the bill to it as required by this provision. If on the tenth day the members and officers were absent, the Governor would have until the first day of their next assembling to return the bill with his objections. To be required to act there must be an organized body in session, at the place holding its sessions."

Applying the decisions of the courts other than that of Illinois to the facts presented by you it would follow that the resolution should have been returned to the House by leaving it with some proper officer of the House, or on the Speaker's desk, or in some way that would have divested the Governor of the possession of the resolution on or before the 4th day of April. On the other hand, applying the Illinois decision to the facts presented, the resolution could not have been returned in the way above stated, but should have been returned at the assembling of the House on the 7th day of April.

The return of the resolution as appears from your statement of facts, having been made on the 8th day of April, would manifestly be outside the sanction of all the decisions ; so it is perhaps unnecessary to consider which line of decisions on this point is correct in principle.

On your statement of facts and not considering the possible

existence of other facts not included therein, and because of the decisions of other states on questions and under conditions almost identical with those submitted by you, I am of the opinion that Joint Resolution No. 25 became a law before it was returned to the House on the 8th day of April, and that the return of the resolution on that day and the action of the House taken on its return in no way affected its validity.

It would, however, seem to be my duty to call your attention to one possible fact, which, if it exists, is of great importance, and to which your statement makes no reference. In the official record of the recent Constitutional Convention, Vol. 7, pages 2302-2309 inclusive, there are suggestions of a construction which in practice has been placed at times on Section 12, Article Fourth. It is not within your province, nor is it within mine, to determine the existence of the possible fact to which I refer; the courts alone are clothed with that authority. If, however, it is a fact that for a long period of time the executive department of this State has acted on a construction of the Constitution by which construction the Governor when exercising the veto power has held bills for three legislative days, and if during that long period of time the legislative department has acquiesced in such a construction, then the proposition that such actual construction might prevail as against a legal construction is supported by a practically unbroken array of authorities of which it is necessary to cite only a few.

In Stuart vs. Laird, 1 Cranch (U. S.), 299, it was held "that a practical construction placed upon a constitutional provision by the judiciary acting under it was a contemporary interpretation of the most forcible nature and conclusive of the legality of the practice."

In the People vs. La Salle, 100 Ill., 495, the court, quoting with approval the case just referred to, said:

"Of similar weight and dignity is the construction placed by the political department of the government upon constitutional provisions under which they are charged with acting."

Endlich on Interpretation of Statutes, Section 527.
Solomon vs. Commissioners, 41 Ga., 157.

Cooley's Constitutional Limitations (6 ed.), pages 81-86, and cases there cited.

The question in the first paragraph of your request for an opinion as to whether "there is now in legal existence a town of South Norwalk in this State" is answered by Section 8 of Joint Resolution No. 25, which provides that the resolution shall take effect on the first Monday of October, A.D. 1903.

It is true that the attorney-general has no power to declare what the law is. That attribute belongs to the courts. I can give you merely an opinion, which, at the best, is but an attempted forecast of what a court would probably declare the law to be on a given state of facts. The value of any opinion must depend not only on its embodying a correct statement of the law, but also on its being based on the same facts that are before the court when the court declares the law.

WILLIAM A. KING,
Attorney-General.

SENTENCE FOR OFFENSE COMMITTED PRIOR TO THE INDETERMINATE SENTENCE ACT.

A sentence to prison for an offense committed prior to the passage of the "Indeterminate Sentence Act" is subject to the laws in force at the date when the offense was committed.

HARTFORD, September 14, 1903.

HON. ALBERT GARVIN, Warden of the Connecticut State Prison.

My Dear Sir: — You submit to me the case of a prisoner sentenced to the State Prison on March 4, 1903, for the term of one year, for an offense committed June 16, 1898, and request me to advise you whether or not the provisions of section 3341 of the General Statutes, Revision of 1888, relating to deduction of time for good behavior, apply to this case.

In my opinion the provisions of the section referred to apply in every case where the offense was committed on or before the 31st day of July, 1901. I, therefore, advise you that, in the case submitted by you, the prisoner is entitled to the deduction for good behavior under the conditions set forth in section 3341 of the Revision of 1888.

WILLIAM A. KING,
Attorney-General.

JUDICIAL SALARIES AND EXPENSES.

Chapter 163 of the Public Acts of 1903, fixing the salary of the judges of the Superior Court and of the Supreme Court as their "terms of office shall hereafter begin," does not conflict with article twenty-four of the Constitution forbidding the increase of the compensation of any public officer during his continuance in office.

Chapter 137 of the Acts of 1903, increasing the amount allowed the judges of said courts for expenses, is not in violation of article twenty-four of the Constitution.

HARTFORD, September 30, 1903.

HON. WILLIAM E. SEELEY, Comptroler.

My Dear Sir: — You submit to me two questions, of which this is the first:

"Does the statute fixing the salary of judges of the Superior Court at $6,000 a year violate the provisions of Article 24 of Amendments to the Constitution?"

I quote the Article of the Constitution as well as the statute (Chapter 163 of the Public Acts of 1903), to which you refer:

Article Twenty-Four: "Neither the General Assembly, nor any County, City, Borough, Town or School District, shall have power to pay or grant any extra compensation to any public officer, employee, agent or servant, or increase the compensation of any public officer or employee, to take effect during the continuance in office of any person whose salary might be increased thereby, or increase the pay or compensation of any public contractor above the amount specified in the contract."

Chapter 163: "The chief justice of the Supreme Court of Errors, each associate justice of said court, and each judge of the Superior Court, as their respective terms of office shall hereafter begin, shall receive annual salaries as follows: The chief justice of the Supreme Court of Errors, six thousand five hundred dollars; each associate justice of said court and each judge of the Superior Court six thousand dollars."

1st. The act, in precise language, contemplates an increase applying only to future terms of office. It is difficult to see how Article Twenty-Four could be so construed as to extend its prohibition to a future term of office unless by reason of the words "continuance in office." The Supreme Court in Smith *vs*. The City of Waterbury, 54 Conn. 176, holds, however, that by the words "continuance in office" the Constitution means continuing in office under one appointment.

The decision cited would seem to determine the answer to your question so far as Article Twenty-Four is concerned.

The prohibition, if it extends to the subject matter you lay before me, applies only to terms of office which were actually existent at the time the Act took effect.

I advise you, therefore, that the act clearly avoids the prohibition which your question assumes to be embraced in Article Twenty-Four, and is not in conflict with that Article.

Your second question is this:

"If that amendment includes the constitutional officers of the State, whose offices, terms of office and mode of appointment are subject to legislative changes, does the Act increasing the allowance for expenses of the judges of the Superior Court violate its provisions?"

The act to which this inquiry relates is Chapter 137 of the Public Acts of 1903. This is the fourth act, in point of time, on this subject. The following is so much of these Acts as is material, and the order in which they were passed:

Chapter 114 of the Acts of 1881, Section 2:

"Each judge of the Supreme Court of Errors and of the Superior Court thereafter appointed, when holding a regular or special term of said court, shall be allowed his necessary expenses therefor, to be paid to him by the Sheriff of the county in which he shall act, and taxed in the bills of said court, but no such judge shall receive for such expenses in the aggregate more than five hundred dollars a year."

Chapter 78 of the Acts of 1883:

" Each judge of the Supreme Court of Errors and of the Superior Court, who is or may be entitled to receive his necessary expenses while engaged in official duty, shall be allowed for such expenses not exceeding five hundred dollars per annum, to be paid quarterly by the Treasurer upon the audit of the Comptroller, and as part of the expenses so to be paid, the judges of the Supreme Court of Errors hereafter appointed shall be allowed their necessary expenses while attending their meetings for official purposes."

Chapter 29 of the Acts of 1893, Section 1 :

" There shall be allowed the chief justice of the Supreme Court of Errors, and each judge of the Supreme and Superior Courts, for their necessary expenses while engaged in official duty, the sum of one thousand dollars annually, to be paid quarterly by the Treasurer."

Chapter 137 of the Acts of 1903:

" There shall be allowed to the chief justice of the Supreme Court of Errors, to each associate justice of said court, and to each judge of the Superior Court, the sum of five hundred dollars per annum, to be paid quarterly, for their necessary expenses, in addition to the sum now allowed by law for such purpose; said allowance to take effect from and after the passage of this Act."

You will thus see that the Acts of 1881 and 1883 excluded from their operation a judge who was serving a term of office to which he had been appointed prior to the passage of the Act of 1881.

The Acts of 1893 and 1903 make no such discrimination; they apply to all the judges irrespective of the date of appointment or the beginning of the term of office, and include those in office at the date when the respective Acts take effect.

The distinction between these two earlier and two later Acts is striking. The earlier Acts strongly indicate that the General Assembly considered Article Twenty-Four of the

Constitution as prohibiting an allowance for expenses to take effect during an existing term of office. The later Acts just as strongly indicate that the General Assembly construed the amendment as permitting such allowance to be made.

The last two acts seem to be based on two propositions:

(1) That the terms " salary " and " compensation " as used in Article Twenty-Four of the Constitution do not include an allowance for expenses.

(2) That in authorizing this allowance the General Assembly is not limited to the adoption of a mode of procedure by which the actual expenses of each judge should be ascertained.

As to the correctness of the first of these two propositions the authorities are not numerous, and in only a few cases are they applicable.

Throop on Public Officers, Section 466, says that a Constitutional provision against increasing or diminishing the salaries of particular officers does not " prevent an allowance for expenses."

Sniffen vs. New York, 4 Sand., 196, holds:

" But the term ' salary ' of itself imports a compensation for personal services, and not the repayment of moneys expended in the discharge of the duties of the office."

To the same effect is the decision of the California Supreme Court in Kirkwood vs. Soto, 87 Cal., 394, where it is held that an Article of the Constitution forbidding the compensation of any officer being increased during his term of office applies to the compensation for services to be rendered, and does not forbid an allowance for the incidental expenses of the office.

I entertain little if any doubt that the first proposition, embodied in the Acts of 1893 and 1903, is correct.

The second proposition may be subject to the possible criticism that, to the extent that the allowance for expenses exceeds the actual expenses, it is an increase of salary or compensation. It is hardly necessary to elaborate arguments against this criticism. It would not seem reasonable, however, that the validity of the act should depend on whether in each case the amount of the allowance was actually expended. While, if this were the test, I do not say that in one case the act might be invalid and in another perfectly valid, yet it is apparent that the facts on which the criticism is based might be present in one case and totally and properly absent in another. Illustrations will readily suggest themselves which would, I think, show the somewhat uncertain, if not absurd, nature of such a test.

In my opinion the real test of the proposition is this: Is the act reasonable as to the amount, and is its object what it purports to be and not a guise under which salary or compensation is increased? The General Assembly by passing the act declared the amount reasonable, and only so far as the constitutionality of the act is concerned is this question reviewable. If, in that aspect, it is my duty to pass on the reasonableness of the amount, then in my opinion the Act is reasonable as to the amount, and fairly and reasonably adapted to the object which it purports to attain.

That the object of the act is what it purports, — to provide for expenses and not to make an indirect increase of salary or compensation, — is clearly shown by the action of the General Assembly in passing chapter 137 of the Acts of 1903, quoted in the opinion in response to your first question. The General Assembly there felt free to increase the salary by the addition of $2,000 to take effect at the beginning of each new term of office. The allowance for expenses, however, whether the salary is $6,000, or $4,000, remains the same, $1,500. This would seem to be conclusive that the General Assembly considered $1,500 a proper and reasonable sum for expenses, even if the salary was fixed at $6,000.

In considering this entire matter one cannot forget the general rule applicable. This rule is stated by Judge Ellsworth in Hartford Bridge Co. *vs.* Union Ferry Co., 29 Conn., 210, in these words:

" It is, however, a well settled principle of judicial construction, that before an act of the legislature ought to be declared unconstitutional, its repugnance to the provisions or necessary implications of the Constitution should be manifest, and free from all reasonable doubt."

In my opinion the Act increasing the allowance for expenses of the judges does not conflict with the Constitutional amendment to which you refer.

I am very respectfully,

WILLIAM A. KING,
Attorney-General.

SAVINGS BANK INVESTMENTS.

By the provisions of Chapter 147, of the Public Acts of 1903, the so-called St. Louis terminal bonds became a legal investment for Connecticut savings banks.

HARTFORD, October 26, 1903.

HON. CHARLES H. NOBLE and HON. GEORGE F. KENDALL, Bank Commissioners.

Gentlemen: — Chapter 147 of the Public Acts of 1903 amends Section 3428 of the General Statutes by inserting in the list of legal investments for savings banks the following bonds: " Terminal Railroad Association of St. Louis general mortgage refunding four per centum sinking fund gold bonds of 1953, and in the mortgage bonds heretofore issued, which said general mortgage bonds are to retire at maturity; St. Louis, Iron Mountain & Southern Railroad Company, River and Gulf Division, first mortgage four per centum bonds, due May 1, 1933; Buffalo & Susquehanna Railroad Company first mortgage four per centum gold bonds, due in 1951; and the general or consolidated mortgage bonds of the Louisville & Nashville Railroad Company."

As a result of your investigations I understand that you are satisfied that the last three bonds above named are legal investments, and that the request for my opinion includes only the terminal bonds.

The act in question is somewhat lengthy. It is the resultant of an act originally well defined in purpose, amended so repeatedly and diversely that its present meaning has become to some extent a matter of considerable doubt. That portion of the act from which the uncertainty arises as to the terminal bonds appears on its last page, after the names of all bonds and railroad corporations, and reads as follows:

"No bond of any railroad corporation named in this section shall be a legal investment for a savings bank when such corporation, or the system of which it is a part, shall fail to pay dividends on all of its capital stock."

As there are other restrictions or qualifications scattered through the act, I will, for purposes of convenience, refer to that which I have quoted as "Restriction A." Whether "Restriction A" is a general restriction, applying to the bonds of every railroad corporation named in the act, becomes a material question. On its face, it is true, the restriction appears to be general. An analysis of the act, however, strongly indicates that it is not a general restriction, and neither applies nor was intended to apply, as a qualification preceding admission, to the bonds of every railroad corporation named in the act.

There are four or five classes of bonds set forth in the act. One class, for example, is made a legal investment "provided" (among other qualifications) "that in every case such company shall have paid each year for a period of not less than five years next previous to such investment . . . dividends of not less than four per cent. per annum upon its entire capital stock outstanding."

Now, argument seems hardly necessary to show that "Restriction A" does not necessarily or even naturally apply as a qualification for admission to that class of bonds, because (1) the dividend-payment qualification has been already affixed to those bonds, and (2) such dividend qualification has been fixed at four per cent. per annum, while "Restriction A" has no limit on the per cent. that is to be paid.

There is at least one other class of bonds set forth in the act which, it is demonstrably clear, is unaffected by it, as a qualification for admission.

If, then, "Restriction A" is not general, and does not apply as a qualification preceding admission to every bond in the act, to what bonds, if any, does it apply as such qualification? And if it does not apply at all as a qualification preceding admission, what is its probable object and meaning?

"Restriction A" was made part of the statute in 1901. At the same session the legislature amended the statute by authorizing investments in what is termed "securities." It was a new word, so far as this statute is concerned, and, under this heading, the legislature admitted as legal investments specific issues of bonds of. certain railroad corporations. Hitherto the bonds admitted had not been specifically described as to the particular issue, the date of maturity, and the interest bearing rate. These "securities," however, were all thus minutely described. For instance, the first bond named in this class was thus described: "Central Railroad Company of New Jersey, general mortgage five per centum gold bonds, due July 1, 1987." In other words, the legislature, under the term "securities," made a selection of particular issues of bonds instead of a selection of the bonds of particular railroads or groups of railroads; and this legislative selection seems to have been based on the real or apparent strength of the particular issue of bonds, rather than on the general financial strength of the corporations issuing the bonds as measured by some of the standards appearing in the act relative to some classes of bonds previously admitted. Thus the five year four per cent. dividend record, as a qualification preceding admission, was wholly discarded, so far as these "securities" were concerned; so also the qualification that the capital stock must be equal to at least one-third of the total mortgage indebtedness of the corporation was thrown aside. In short, these bonds denominated "securities" were confessedly admitted as legal investments, and to continue as legal investments, subject only to the limitations embodied in "Restriction A."

As a fact, however, and it seems to me a very important fact, every one of these "securities" so admitted was issued by a corporation that was paying dividends on all its capital stock at the time when the "securities" were admitted.

Now, bearing in mind that "Restriction A" was enacted as

part of this statute at the time these "securities" were admitted, that the "securities" were those of corporations all at
that time paying dividends at varying rates, that the "securities" were confessedly without restriction or qualification of
any kind except so far as imposed by "Restriction A," and the
probable and natural meaning, purpose, and object, of that restriction becomes comparatively clear. "Restriction A" says
that "no bond of any railroad corporation named in this act
shall be a legal investment . . . *when* such corporation
shall fail to pay dividends . . ." This, it seems to me, is
not necessarily a qualification *preceding* admission; it is rather
a limitation on bonds already admitted, determining when the
privileges arising from admission shall cease.

Every corporation issuing these "securities" being a dividend payer at the time the "securities" were admitted, there
could be no reason or necessity for inserting "Restriction A"
as a qualification preceding admission. This is especially
significant when you remember that the "securities" were
admitted and "Restriction A" enacted at practically the same
time. In my opinion "Restriction A," when enacted, in 1901,
meant that the corporations hitherto admitted must keep up to
the dividend paying capacity and performance existing at the
date of admission, or their bonds which had been admitted
would cease to be a legal investment. The restriction operated
in the future, after the bonds had been admitted. Its purpose
was to *serve as a test of removal from the list of those admitted, — not as a qualification preceding admission.* The
words "shall fail to pay dividends" are equivalent to "shall
discontinue, or cease to pay, dividends." In the case of bonds
admitted as the "securities" were admitted, without the safe-
guards thrown around some of the earlier bonds, this construction of "Restriction A" would seem natural and reasonable.
So construed it would mean exactly this: Corporations which
are not subject to the special dividend paying qualification for
admission (as, for instance, the five year four per cent.
qualification), whose bonds were admitted when the corporation was *in fact* paying dividends, must continue up to the
standard on which they were admitted; if they "shall fail"

to keep up to that standard, " Restriction A" operates and removes from the list the bonds of such corporation so failing.

Until the session of 1903 no bond of any railroad corporation had been inserted in the list of legal investments unless, (1) the corporation had qualified prior to admission under specified dividend tests set forth in the act, or, (2) unless the corporation, although not qualifying under specific tests as to dividends, was, *as a fact*, a dividend payer at the time of admission. " Restriction A," construed as above, would clearly apply to the latter class of corporations; whether it applies to the former class is not material, for their own specific dividend tests would render " Restriction A" unnecessary.

In 1903 the legislature added the bonds of the Terminal Railroad Association of St. Louis to the class known as " securities." This corporation was not a dividend payer, never had been, and there is no evidence that it ever will be. It becomes important to discover the intent of the legislature in inserting the terminal bonds in the list of legal investments. Was it intended that these bonds should become an investment without limitation, or was it intended that they should be subject, in some way, to the limitations set forth in " Restriction A," which was left in the act?

In construing an act to determine the intent, the question always is, what is the meaning of what the legislature has said, and not what did the legislature actually mean to say? In determining this intent, however, the general object of the statute, its " history and progress," and the nature of the subject-matter with which it deals, are legitimate and competent evidence.

Thus, in determining the intent in this act, one may properly consider the general object of the act, its history, and its subject-matter, including the nature of the terminal association and its bonds.

The mortgage securing the bonds and the guaranty agreements with the fourteen proprietary corporations comprise hundreds of printed pages, and it is possible to give only a brief summary of their import.

The terminal association is the product of the merger of

two corporations. It is, in my opinion, a·railroad corporation, although, as its name indicates, it owns very extensive terminal. properties and facilities, far in excess of what its own railway business requires. Its issued capital stock is somewhat less than $1,500,000, which is owned in equal shares by fourteen railway companies, including the Missouri Pacific, Illinois Central, Burlington & Quincy, Louisville & Nashville, and others.

Under a guaranty agreement between these fourteen companies so holding the stock, the terminal association, and the trustees, each of these companies binds itself forever to make use of the properties of the terminal association for all passenger and freight traffic within its control through, to, and from St. Louis, and destined to cross the Mississippi at St. Louis; and further agrees that the tariff rates of the terminal association shall be so fixed by it as to insure the production at all times of sufficient revenue to enable it to meet and discharge the interest on all its bonds, debt, rentals, sinking fund installments, taxes, and all expenses of every nature incurred in the maintenance, operation, and renewal of its system and properties. Under this agreement each of the proprietary companies, also to the extent of its proportionate interest (onefourteenth (in the terminal association, guarantees the payment of all interest on the terminal bonds, and the payment of the installments of the sinking fund.

Now, bearing in mind that the terminal association never has paid dividends on its stock, there is surely nothing in the nature of the corporation or its bonds, as above outlined, that would indicate that it was to become a dividend payer. The fourteen holding companies practically fix the charges against themselves for using the terminal facilities; if dividends were paid, out of the revenue thus determined, they would go back to the companies from whose treasuries they had come in the shape of charges. Moreover, it is a presumption of law that a condition once shown to exist continues to exist until evidence to the contrary appears. I think it is clear, from this legitimate evidence, that the law-making power, when inserting the terminal bonds, considered, and will, by the law, be presumed to have considered, the terminal association as a non-dividend paying railroad corporation. If the legislature in voting to insert the bonds in the list, and the executive in approving the act, did so consider it, why did they insert the bonds in the list at all unless they intended to make them a legal investment, irrespective of any question as to dividend payments?

The law presumes that the law-making power knew the nature of the terminal association, the way in which its stock was held, the sources of its income, and the fact that it was a non-dividend paying corporation; and it is difficult to imagine what the law-making power could have intended by naming the terminal bonds in the list, other than to make the bonds of a non-dividend paying corporation a legal investment. If this was not intended why were the bonds named at all? They were engaged in naming bonds that were to be legal investments, — not in naming bonds which were not to be legal investments.

The fact is probably nowhere doubted that the legislature intended to make the terminal bonds a legal investment irrespective of any dividend restriction. It did not seem to me, however, to be legally permissible to find that intent other than from the legitimate sources which have been above indicated. From these sources of legal evidence of the intent, — the general object of the act, its subject matter, and the nature of the bonds, — I am satisfied that the law-making power intended to admit the terminal bonds without reference to any dividend qualification or restriction whatsoever. As previous legislatures had, in relation to certain bonds, discarded qualifications previously thought necessary, so the legislature of 1903 discarded the dividend paying capacity so far as it related to the terminal bonds. Whether the guaranty contract connected with the terminal bonds equals the previous dividend paying restriction as a safeguard, or test of excellence in a bond, may be a matter of opinion. The legislature, however, by its decision, has closed that discussion, so far as the terminal bonds are concerned.

Does "Restriction A," against the expressed intent of the

legislature, exclude the terminal bonds? Construed as I have above construed it, — as not a qualification for admission at all, but purely a restriction intended to remove from the list of investments bonds of corporations *admitted as dividend payers,* but subsequently failing to keep up to that standard, — so construed, it would not exclude the terminal bonds. If, on the other hand, "Restriction A" means that the bonds of no non-dividend paying corporation shall be an investment, and if that is the only construction that can be fairly and reasonably given to it, then it would exclude the terminal bonds. To me it seems, irrespective of the result, in view of the history and analysis of the act, that the former is the natural and true construction of "Restriction A." In construing an act, however, if two constructions are fairly and reasonably possible, we ought to look at the results arising from each. The one construction of "Restriction A" effectuates the intent of the legislature. It gives force to all parts of the act. The other construction defeats the undoubted intent of the legislature. It does more than that. It reduces the legislation concerning the terminal bonds to an absurdity. On one page the bonds are admitted, on the next page, while possessing every attribute with which they were endowed when admitted, they would be excluded. Such incongruous results ought not to be imputed to the language of the act if they can be fairly and reasonably avoided.

Let me quote the language of our Supreme Court in passing on questions analogous to this:

In Brown's Appeal, 72 Conn., 150, the court, in deciding against an alleged literal construction of a statute, says:

"Such a construction leads to results absurd and impracticable, which the legislature could not have intended. This of itself is sufficient to mark the construction as wrong. The letter of a statute cannot prevail against the plainly indicated intent of the legislature. Bridgeport *vs.* Hubbell, 5 Conn., 237, 243; Richmondville Mfg. Co. *vs.* Prall, 9 id., 487, 495; Rawson *vs.* The State, 19 id., 292, 299."

State *vs.* Travelers Ins. Co., 73 Conn., 277:

" When occasion demands, the court cannot shrink from its duty in discovering the real purpose of any legislation."

Rawson *vs.* The State, 19 Conn., 299:

" All statutes, whether remedial or penal, should be construed according to the apparent intention of the legislature, to be gathered from the language used, connected with the subject of legislation, and so that the entire language shall have effect, if it can, without defeating the obvious design and purpose of the law. And in doing this, the application of common sense to the language is not to be excluded."

Andrews *vs.* R. R. Co., 60 Conn., 297:

" The purpose of the statute ought not to be sacrificed to its letter."

Miles *vs.* Strong, 68 Conn., 287:

" It is a safe and wholesome rule, that where an act of the legislature admits of two constructions, one valid and the other invalid, courts should adopt the former and uphold the statute, if it may be done by any reasonable interpretation, though it may not be the most obvious."

Camp *vs.* Rogers, 44 Conn., 298:

" If, upon the construction we have been considering, the law in question would be void, or even of doubtful validity, it is our duty to find, if we are able, some other construction that will relieve it of this difficulty. If a law can be upheld by a reasonable construction it ought to be done . . . It is a rule of very frequent application that courts will be astute in giving a construction to a statute that shall save it from invalidity."

I advise you, that, in my opinion, the terminal bonds are made a legal investment for savings banks by the provisions of Chapter 147 of the Public Acts of 1903.

I am very respectfully,

WILLIAM A. KING,

Attorney-General.

STATE BOARD OF AGRICULTURE.

Circumstances and conditions under which the State Board of Agriculture may withhold certificate entitling agricultural societies to money from the State.

HARTFORD, November 13, 1903.

HON. JAMES F. BROWN, Secretary State Board of Agriculture, North Stonington, Conn.:

My Dear Sir: — I am in receipt of the following communication from you:

NORTH STONINGTON, Nov. 5, 1903.

HON. WM. A. KING,
  Attorney-General,
    Willimantic, Conn.

DEAR SIR: —

At a meeting of this board, Nov. 4th, the secretary was directed to obtain the opinion of the attorney-general as to the powers of this board by its secretary, under the provisions of Sec. 4400, Gen. Statutes, Rev. of 1902, to withhold the certificate on which the comptroller's order is drawn on the treasurer, for the alleged reason that the provisions of Sec. 4401 have not been complied with. In other words, can the secretary of this board question the returns of an agricultural society, made by its president, secretary, and treasurer, in compliance with Sec. 4400 above referred to, on the complaint of any one that Sec. 4401 has been violated?

Very respectfully,

JAMES F. BROWN, *Secy.*

Section 4400 provides in substance that a statement of the amount of premiums, and the object for which they have been paid, sworn to by the president, secretary, and treasurer of an agricultural society, shall be forwarded to the secretary of the State Board of Agriculture. The secretary of said board " shall thereupon certify to the Comptroller the amount to which each society is entitled, and proper orders on the State Treasurer shall be drawn for payment of the same."

I quote sections 4401 and 4402:

Section 4401: " No part of any building or grounds within the enclosure in which is held a fair of any incorporated agricultural society shall be leased for the sale of spirit-

uous or intoxicating liquors, the running of wheel-pools, so
called, or the unlawful practice of any games of chance, nor
shall any right or privilege be granted to any person to
carry on such sale or games within such inclosure during the
continuance of such fair."

Section 4402: "No such society shall be entitled to its
usual appropriation from the State treasury unless the president, secretary, and treasurer thereof shall make oath in its
annual statement to the secretary of the State Board of Agriculture that the provisions of section 4401 have not been violated with their knowledge and consent."

The obvious purpose of the last section is to withhold
the State's money from an agricultural society which has violated any provision of section 4401, with the knowledge and
consent of the president, secretary, or treasurer.

It is the duty of the secretary of the State Board of Agriculture to certify to the Comptroller, in accordance with Section 4400, when the statement embodying the oath as set forth
in section 4402 has been filed with him; unless he is satisfied
by competent and sufficient evidence that the sworn statement
is untrue, — that is, that there has been a violation of the provisions of section 4401 with the knowledge and consent of
one of the three officers named.

That he is satisfied by such evidence, as I have indicated,
that section 4401 has been violated, is not enough to justify
him in withholding the certificate. He must also be satisfied
that such violation occurred with the knowledge and consent
of either the president, the treasurer, or the secretary. The
sworn statement referred to in section 4402 carries with it the
presumption that it is true, and he ought to accept such sworn
statement and give the certificate, unless he is convinced that
the sworn statement is untrue. If, however, the secretary of
the board is so convinced by the evidence, I advise you that,
in my opinion, it would be his duty to withhold the certificate.

It is not feasible to lay down a general rule by which in
each case you could safely determine what constitutes competent and sufficient evidence. If there is a case in which
evidence has been submitted to you proving, or tending to

prove, to your satisfaction that, on the construction of the law as above stated, you ought not to issue a certificate, it would be the duty of the Attorney-General, if you so desire, to consider the evidence with you, and, if you wish, to advise with you in relation thereto.

I am very respectfully,

WILLIAM A. KING,
Attorney-General.

POWERS OF BOARD OF PAROLE.

Until the expiration of the maximum term of a sentence the board of parole may issue its order for the return of a prisoner who has violated his parole.

HARTFORD, January 15, 1904.

HON. THOMAS D. WELLS, Secretary of the Board of Parole, Hartford, Conn.: —

My Dear Sir: — I have before me your communication of January 9th reading as follows:

"On October 15, 1901, Philip Heitchman was sentenced to State Prison from Windham County for a term of from one to three years. On July 7, 1903, he was conditionally released on parole. Last week he was arrested at Attleboro, Mass., charged with committing an offense in that place on November 29th last, and he is now in a Massachusetts jail awaiting trial. If he is kept in Massachusetts until after the expiration of the three year period of his maximum term of imprisonment in Connecticut has expired, can the time between the violation of his parole and his reimprisonment in this State be deducted from his term of imprisonment, or does the authority which the Board of Parole has over him lapse on October 15, 1904, the calendar date of the termination of his maximum sentence?"

I advise you, that, in my opinion, the power of the Board of Parole to make the order or request for the return of Heitchman will expire at the termination of the maximum term of imprisonment to which he was sentenced. If, however, the Board of Parole, before the termination of such maximum sentence, issues its request or order for his return, he may be retaken and returned on that order so issued, although such retaking and return is not effectuated until after the date of the expiration of his maximum sentence.

Assuming, for instance, that the order for his return was issued on January 15, 1904, and the paroled prisoner was not returned until after October 15, 1904 (the date of the expiration of his maximum sentence), he would then, under the statute, be obliged to serve nine months after he was returned, although that return was subsequent to the expiration of his maximum term of imprisonment.

The period of time equal to the unexpired term of his sentence, at the date of the request or order for his return, constitutes the period that he would have to serve when returned, even though such return takes place after the expiration of his maximum sentence. This, of course, implies that the board may make the order or request for his return at any time before the expiration of that maximum sentence, but not after such maximum term has expired.

I am very respectfully,

WILLIAM A. KING,
Attorney-General.

LIFE INSURANCE.

The assumption by one life insurance company of the risks of another does not constitute reinsurance, within the meaning of our statutes.

HARTFORD, January 28, 1904.

HON. THERON UPSON, Insurance Commissioner, Hartford, Conn.

My Dear Sir: — Your communication relative to the Hartford Life Insurance Company and its proposed action is before me, together with that of Mr. Sperry to you.

Section 3557 of the General Statutes forbids an insurance company incorporated by or organized under the laws of this State, to consolidate or amalgamate with any other company, reinsure its risks, or any part thereof, with any other company, or assume or reinsure the whole or any portion of the risks of any other company except as provided in section 3558.

The proposed action of the Hartford Life Insurance Company with the Metropolitan Life Insurance Company does not, if effectuated, constitute consolidation, amalgamation, or reinsurance of risks or any part thereof. The term reinsurance has a well settled meaning. Bouvier's Law Dictionary defines reinsurance as follows:

"Insurance effected by an underwriter upon a subject against certain risks, with another underwriter, on the same subject, against all or a part of the same risks, not exceeding the same amount. In the original insurance, he is the insurer; in the second, the assured. His object in reinsurance is to protect himself against the risks which he has assumed. There is no privity of contract between the original assured and the reinsurer, and the reinsurer is under no liability to such original assured. 3 Kent. 227; 1 Phill. Ins. Sec. 78 a, 404; 20 Barb. 468, 23 Pa. 250; 9 Ind. 443; 13 La Ann. 246. See Beach, Ins. 1283; Pars. Mari. Ins. 301."

The proposed contract of assumption to be entered into between the Metropolitan Life Insurance Company and the present holders of policies in the Hartford Life Insurance Company, as set forth in Mr. Sperry's communication, reads as follows:

"The Metropolitan Life Insurance Company hereby assumes this policy as its own, provided the same is in force by its terms and agrees with the owner thereof to perform the same in place of the Hartford Life Insurance Company, and the owner of this policy hereby agrees to accept the Metropolitan Life Insurance Company as a party to this policy in place and release of the Hartford Life Insurance Company, and to pay all premiums to the Metropolitan Life Insurance Company. This contract is placed upon this policy by agreement of the owner thereof."

You will see that this is not reinsurance of the risks of the Hartford Company by the Metropolitan Company, within the meaning of the term reinsurance as used in the statute. There is nothing in section 3557 to prohibit the assumption of risks by a life insurance company, unless the company so assuming has been incorporated by or organized under the laws of this State. The Metropolitan Life Insurance Company was not organized by or under the laws of this State.

In 1893 the Metropolitan Life Insurance Company assumed the policies of the People's Industrial Insurance Company of Norwich, under an agreement with the policy-holders of the latter company, — substantially that proposed in the present case. (See Annual Report of the Insurance Commissioner for 1893, Part II, Page xxiv).

I advise you, that, in my opinion, the proposed action of the Metropolitan Life Insurance Company in assuming the policies in the way above set forth, is not in conflict with the provisions of sections 3557 and 3558, and that you have no duty in the-premises.

I am very respectfully,

WILLIAM A. KING,
Attorney-General.

PUBLIC SCHOOLS.

The statute providing that public schools shall be maintained "thirty-six weeks in each year" excludes holidays falling within a school week.

HARTFORD, February 18, 1904.

HON. W. E. SEELEY, Comptroller, Hartford, Conn.

My Dear Sir: — I have before me the following communication from you dated February 16, 1904:

"Section 2130 of the General Statutes prescribes that 'public schools shall be maintained for at least thirty-six weeks in each year in every town and school district. No town shall receive any money from the State treasury for any district unless the school therein has been kept during the time herein required.'

"As payment devolves upon the Comptroller, a construction has recently been requested from this department.

"I therefore inquire from you how many days constitute a week under this statute, and whether such days as are designated as legal holidays by Section 4364 can be deducted from the same, also such days as are allowed by custom for teachers to visit other schools?"

I advise you, that, in my opinion, the term "thirty-six weeks" used in the statute means thirty-six weeks of five days each, less such deductions as should be made. Thirty-six school weeks do not necessarily include one hundred and eighty days on which the school must be kept open. Thus the school week commencing February 22, 1904 (a legal holiday), will consist of only four days. The requirement of the statute is fulfilled when the school is taught for thirty-six weeks of five days each, less such days as should be deducted therefrom, including in such deduction legal holidays occurring within the school week.

In reply to your second question as to whether days should be deducted which are allowed by custom for the visitation of other schools: If such custom exists, and is sanctioned by the authorities having control and supervision of the school, then such days should be deducted from the thirty-six weeks of five days each.

You will not understand that the above instances include all the deductions which may be legally made. Conditions may exist which would justify the deduction of other days. The language of the Supreme Court of Michigan on a different but somewhat analogous question, (School District *vs.* Gage, 39 Mich., 484), expresses the law as applicable to this subject:

" In regard to deductions for holidays we are of the opinion that school management should always conform to those decent usages which recognize the propriety of omitting to hold public exercises on recognized holidays; and that it is not lawful to impose forfeitures or deductions for such proper suspension of labor. Schools should conform to what may fairly be expected of all institutions in civilized communities. All contracts for teaching during periods mentioned must be construed, of necessity, as subject to such days of vacation, and public policy as well as usage requires that there should be no penalty laid upon such observances."

I am very respectfully,

WILLIAM A. KING,

Attorney-General.

CORPORATION ORGANIZED IN CONNECTION WITH A ROMAN CATHOLIC CHURCH.

In order to exercise the powers conferred by law on a corporation organized in connection with a Roman Catholic church or congregation, the certificate of organization must be signed by the bishop, the vicar-general, the pastor, and two laymen, as required by Chapter 117 of the Public Acts of 1903.

HARTFORD, May 20, 1904.

HON. CHARLES G. R. VINAL, Secretary of State.

Dear Sir: — *In re* "Articles of Association of St. Joseph's Polish Roman Catholic Congregation of Norwich, Conn."

Complying with your request for a written opinion as to whether the above named Articles of Association are in conformity with law I submit the following:

The Articles of Association in question provide for the formation of a religious society to be known as " St. Joseph's Polish Roman Catholic Congregation of Norwich, Conn," whose members shall consist of Roman Catholics and such as shall be hereafter admitted "according to the rules and usages of the Roman Catholic Church and the laws of this State."

The objects of the corporation are not set forth in the Articles, except as they may be inferred. Article VII. provides that the auditors to be appointed shall " control all property, real and personal, of said corporation "; Article XII. that " all moneys collected or received shall be deposited . . . to the credit " of the corporation, while Articles XIV. and XV. are as follows:

"Art. XIV. When ready for the appointment of a Pastor Priest, the Roman Catholic Bishop of the diocese of Hartford shall be informed of the fact and that the members of said congregation are all of Polish nationality, and he shall be respectfully requested and urged to appoint over them a pastor of their own nationality, and said pastor, by virtue of his appointment and without further action of the congregation, shall become and remain, so long as his pastorate continues, a member of the financial and managing committees of the congregation, with all the rights and privileges pertaining thereto.

"Art. XV. When the congregation shall become free from debt, it shall then be governed by eight directors, composed of members of the congregation and elected annually at its regular annual meetings."

As I understand these Articles of Association they constitute an attempt to form a corporation in connection with a Roman Catholic Church for religious purposes in accordance with the doctrines, rules, and usages of that Church; and the corporation so formed is to hold and control the property, real and personal, that it may in any way acquire for those purposes. The formation of the society is evidently based on section 3939 of the General Statutes, which provides that Christians of any denomination may unite to form religious societies, and when so formed for purposes of public religious worship may hold property, etc., after properly filing copies of their Articles of Association as prescribed in section 3940.

The Articles of Association are approved, adopted, and signed by twenty-five members of the said St. Joseph's Polish Roman Catholic Congregation, but are not signed by the Bishop and the Vicar-General of the diocese of Hartford, and the pastor, as provided in section 3989 of the General Statutes as amended by Chapter 117 of the Public Acts of 1903, relating to the formation of a corporation in connection with the Roman Catholic Church.

If there were no statutes other than sections 3939 and 3940 providing for the formation of religious societies, there would be little, if any, doubt that the Articles of Association before me complied with the law. Special provision, however, for the formation of corporations in connection with the Roman Catholic Church is made by sections 3989, 3990, and 3991 as follows:

" Section 3989 (as amended by Ch. 117 of the Public Acts of 1903) : A corporation may be organized in connection with any Roman Catholic Church or congregation in this State, by filing in the office of the Secretary of State a certifi-

cate signed by the Bishop and the Vicar-General of the diocese of Hartford and the pastor and two laymen belonging
to such congregation, stating that they have so organized for
the purposes hereinafter mentioned. Such Bishop, Vicar-
General, and pastor of such congregation shall be members,
ex officio, of such corporation, and upon their death, resigna-
tion, removal or preferment, their successors in office shall
become such members in their stead. The two lay members
shall be appointed annually, in writing, during the month of
January from the lay members of the congregation by a
majority of the *ex officio* members of the corporation, and three
members of the corporation, of whom one shall be a layman,
shall constitute a quorum for the transaction of business.

" Sec. 3990. Such corporation may receive and hold all
property conveyed to it for the purpose of maintaining religious worship according to the doctrine, discipline, and ritual
of the Roman Catholic Church, and for the support of the
educational or charitable institutions of that church; *provided*
that no one incorporated church or congregation shall at any
time possess an amount of property, excepting church buildings, parsonages, schoolhouses, asylums, and cemeteries, the
annual income from which shall exceed three thousand
dollars.

" Sec. 3991. Such corporation shall at all times be subject
to the general laws and discipline of the Roman Catholic
Church, and shall receive and enjoy its franchises as a body
politic, solely for the purposes mentioned in Section 3990;
and upon the violation or surrender of its charter, its property, real and personal, shall vest in the Bishop of the diocese
and his successors, in trust for such congregation, and for
the use and purposes above named."

Our Supreme Court in the case State *ex rel* Barry *vs.*
Getty, 69 Conn., 286, in discussing sections 3989 and 3990
says:

" The law for the Roman Catholics provides merely for
corporations to hold the legal title to the property they may
receive for the purposes named in the statute. . . . Prior
to 1866, when the law was passed, property appropriated to

the uses of the Roman Catholic Church was held in trust by the Bishop, personally; the practical effect of the law is to enable the Bishop to hold the property as a corporation. A careful examination of the sections cited, shows that while there are local corporations connected with local churches or congregations, nevertheless each corporation consists of five members, of whom the Bishop, his Vicar-General, and pastor must form a majority; and section 2094 (now section 3991) provides that whenever the local corporation sees fit to surrender its charter, all the property vests in the Bishop and his successors as a corporation sole."

If the association was formed under the Articles which are before me it would be to all intents and purposes a Roman Catholic Association or Congregation, except so far as holding and controlling its property was concerned. I do not think that it is the intent of the statutes to permit that property to be held other than in the way set forth in sections 3989 and 3990; that is, by a corporation among the members of which shall be the Bishop, Vicar-General, and Pastor.

I therefore advise you that, in my opinion, the Articles of Association in question are not formed in compliance with the provisions of the statutes relative to such associations or corporations.

I am very respectfully,

WILLIAM A. KING,
Attorney-General.

RESERVE FUND OF SURETY COMPANIES.

The "maximum liability" referred to in the statute, on which the reserve fund is to be computed, is the maximum amount, under the terms of the contract, which the surety company would, in any event, be obligated to pay.

HARTFORD, December 6, 1904.

HON. THERON UPSON, Insurance Commissioner, Hartford, Conn.

My Dear Sir: — Replying to your communication of December 1st, *in re* the construction of section 3653 of the General Statutes of Connecticut quoted below:

SECTION 3653. "Every surety company or association chartered by or doing business in this State and having the power to execute or guarantee surety or fidelity bonds or obligations, or guarantee the validity of titles or written instruments, shall at all times keep and maintain a reserve fund for reinsurance equal to two dollars for each one thousand dollars of liability to be estimated upon the maximum liability as expressed in the contracts of such company or association."

In my opinion the phrase "liability to be estimated upon the maximum liability as expressed in the contracts of such company," means and is equivalent to the maximum liability to which the contract binds the company. This is not necessarily the amount of the bond, — but is the maximum amount which the company, by the terms of its contract, would be obligated to pay. If the maximum liability, according to the terms of the contract, is $5,000, and the bond is for the amount of $10,000, the reserve fund to be maintained would be computed on $5,000, and not on $10,000.

Unless the maximum liability is specifically stated in the contract, or stated in such manner that the law would from such statement determine the maximum liability, I do not, as a practical proposition, see how you can assume the maximum liability to be other than the amount of the bond as it appears in the contract.

It is perhaps true that the statute, in its present form, works a hardship, in some instances, on surety companies and associations. It is manifest that the General Assembly, by a slight change in the statute, might eliminate this hardship in the operation of the law and still retain the elements of safety which are apparently the object of the law.

I am very respectfully,

WILLIAM A. KING,

Attorney-General.

SURETY COMPANY.

Amount of capital required as a prerequisite to admission to this State.

HARTFORD, December 12, 1904.

Hon. THERON UPSON, Insurance Commissioner, Hartford, Conn.

My Dear Sir: — The Title Guaranty and Trust Company of Scranton, Pennsylvania, is seeking admission to this State for the purpose of doing the business of surety insurance. It has a capital of $750,000. Its charter authorizes it to do the business of a trust company, and it is engaged in that business as well as that of surety insurance. Its entire capital, by virtue of its charter and by the laws of its own State, is held as the security required by law for the full performance of its duties as a trust company, and is absolutely holden to meet those obligations.

You request me to advise you whether, on the above state of facts, it is your duty to admit the company to this State.

Our statutes demand as prerequisites of admission to do business in this State that a surety company shall be possessed of $250,000 capital, and that such capital to the extent of $100,000 shall be invested in certain securities, deposited with an officer of the State under whose laws the company is incorporated, — as fully set forth in section 3645 of the General Statutes.

In my opinion the capital, $250,000, must be holden as security for the obligations arising solely from the surety business, $100,000 being specifically set aside, as provided in Section 3645. As all the capital of the company in question is subject to the prior claims and obligations which may arise from the trust company business, I advise you that, so far as the capital is concerned, this is not a compliance with our statutes. It is not enough that $100,000 of the capital has been deposited, as provided in section 3645. In addition to that, the company must have at least $150,000 capital as security for defaults arising out of the surety business.

I therefore advise you that the company in question is not entitled to admission to do a surety business in this State, under the facts which you place before me.

If, however, you become satisfied that the company has at least $250,000, including the deposit required by section 3645, in trust, or so placed, that it is to respond solely to the obligations arising out of its surety business, I advise you that, in that event, you would be authorized to admit the company.

I am very respectfully,

WILLIAM A. KING,
Attorney-General.

FRATERNAL INSURANCE SOCIETIES.

A fraternal insurance society, conforming to the laws of our State, is entitled to admission although it does business elsewhere which does not conform to the requirements of our statutes.

HARTFORD, December 23, 1904.

HON. THERON UPSON, Insurance Commissioner, Hartford, Conn.

My Dear Sir: — You submit for my consideration the following:

"May a fraternal beneficiary society organized under the laws of another State or country be admitted to do business in Connecticut if, under the provisions of its articles of incorporation or constitution and by-laws, it issues beneficiary certificates that conflict with the provisions of the fraternal law of this State? I refer more particularly to section 3582, General Statutes, in which the benefits are limited to certain relatives or to persons dependent upon the member of the society. Would the extension of the benefits to parties outside the law's limitation make such a society ineligible for admission here, even if it should issue a special membership certificate in Connecticut limiting the benefits to the classes named in our statutes while still issuing the broader certificates elsewhere?"

It is possible that a strict construction of section 3582 of the General Statutes would prohibit a secret or fraternal society from doing business in this State if it anywhere issued certificates that conflicted with the provisions of our law, although its acts within our State were in perfect conformity to our statute.

Considering, however, the entire chapter relating to secret and fraternal societies, and particularly section 3595, I am satisfied that such is not the intention of the chapter nor necessarily its meaning.

I therefore advise you that if the society does business in this State in compliance with our law it is entitled to admission, even if it does business elsewhere which does not conform to the requirements of section 3582.

I am very respectfully,

WILLIAM A. KING,

Attorney-General.

STATEMENT OF COST OF ASSISTANCE RENDERED THE OFFICE WITHIN THE STATE. PERSONAL AND INCIDENTAL EXPENSES.

1903.			
May 7,	Assistance in preparing opinion, *in re* South Norwalk veto, .	Chas. E. Gross,	$100.00
May 13,	Assistance in preparing opinion, *in re* South Norwalk veto, .	Dwight Loomis,	100.00
June 4,	Clerical services, ...	C. E. Hoadley,	25.00
July 2,	Legal services, pauper cases, .	John H. Buck,	20.00
Sept. 3,	Legal services and expenses in Nettleton's appeal, . . .	Donald T. Warner,	182.50
Nov. 28,	Assistance in Wm. Cook matter,	Chas. E. Perkins,	25.00
Dec. 2,	Preparation and trial of case City of Hartford *v.* Maslen, . .	Charles Phelps,	983.55
1904.			
May 3,	Services in State *v.* Griffin, . .	Frank E. Healy,	50.00
May 11,	Services in Supreme Court in City of Hartford *v.* Maslen, .	Charles Phelps,	190.65
May 23,	Services in Nettleton's appeal, .	Donald T. Warner,	300.00
June 1,	Services in Ferris succession tax,	Michael Kenealy,	50.00
July 13,	Services in Probate Court *in re* succession tax in Mary F. Hopkins estate, ...	E. L. Scofield,	288.00
July 13,	Services in Probate Court for the District of Greenwich, . .	James Walsh,	50.00
Sept. 24,	Searching title to land for the State, ...	Wilbur Halliday,	10.00
Oct. 7,	Legal assistance in Andrus matter, ...	Fred A. Scott,	68.12
		$	2,443.27

Personal and incidental expenses during the year 1903, as per vouchers on file with the Comptroller, ... $255.58

Personal and incidental expenses during the year 1904, as per vouchers on file with the Comptroller, ... 222.97

$477.55

LIBRARY OF THE OFFICE.

Bispham's Principles of Equity,　5th Ed.
Brannon on the Fourteenth Amendment.
Bouvier's Law Dictionary,　.　　Rawle's Revision. 2 Vols.
Connecticut Citations,　.　.　John C. Mitchel.
　　"　　Corporation Law, . 8th Ed.　F. G. Beach.
　　"　　Index — Digest,　.　Andrews & Fowler.
　　"　　Registers,　.　. 1887-1904.
Cook on Life Insurance.
Cooley's Constitutional Limita-
　　tions,　.　.　.　. 6th Ed.
Cooley on Taxation, .　.　. 2d Ed.
Decisions of Comptroller of the Treasury.　　　3 Vols.
Dicey on the Conflict of Laws.
Dill on New Jersey Corpora-
　　tions,　.　.　.　. 3d Ed. — 1901.
Dillon's Municipal Corporations, 4th Ed.
Endlich on the Interpretation of the Statutes.
Extraordinary Relief,　.　.　　T. C. Spelling.　2 Vols.
Foster on the Constitution — Preamble to Impeachment.　Vol. 1.
Index Connecticut Special Laws,　1789-1897.
Index General Statutes of Con-
　　necticut,　.　.　.　. 1889-1893.
Miller on the Constitution of the United States.
Moore on Extradition.　　　　　　　2 Vols.
Noyes on Intercorporate Relations.
Notes on Revised Statutes of
　　U. S.,　.　.　.　.　. 1874-1889, Gould & Tucker.　Vol. 1.
Notes on Revised Statutes of
　　U. S.,　.　.　.　.　. 1889-1897,　"　　　　"　2.
Ostrander on Fire Insurance, . 2d Ed.
Police Powers,　.　.　.　　W. P. Prentice.
Practice Act of Connecticut — Rules and Forms.
　　"　　"　　"　　"　　"　(Annotated 1901).
Public Acts of Connecticut,　. 1889-1901.
Receivers of Corporations,　. 2d Ed.　Gluck & Becker.
Revised Statutes of the United
　　States,　.　.　.　. 2d Ed. — 1878.
Revision of Baldwin's Digest.　　　　　2 Vols.
　　"　　Swift's　　"　　　　　　2　"
Rice on Evidence (Civil).　　　　　　· 2　"

Statutes of the United States of
   America, ...   1897.
Statutes of the United States of
   America, ...   1897-1898.
Stephens' Digest of the Law of
   Evidence, ...   G. E. Beers.
Story on Agency,   .   .   .   9th Ed.
Supplement to the Revised Statutes of the United States, 1874-1891.
   "   "   "   "   "   "   "   1892-1895.
   "   "   "   "   "   "   "   1895-1896.
   "   "   "   "   "   "   "   1896-1897.
The Law of Eminent Domain,   C. F. Randolph.
The New Connecticut Civil Officer.
Tiedeman on Municipal Corporations.
Two Centuries' Growth of American Law.
United States First Comptroller's Decisions (Vols. 3 to 6).
Webster's International Dictionary.
Wharton's Criminal Law, .   .   10th Ed.   2 Vols.
Kirby's Reports,   1785-1788
Root's   "   1764-1793   Vol. 1
   "   "   1793-1798   "   2
Day's   "   1802-1804   "   1
• "   1805-1807   "   2
   "   1807-1809   "   3
                1809-1810   "   4
   "   "   1811-1813   "   5
Connecticut Reports,   1814-1904   (76 Vols.)
Private Laws of Connecticut,   1789-1836, Vols. 1 and 2.
   "   "   "   "   1836-1856,   "   3
   "   "   "   "   1836-1856,   " ,   4
   "   "   "   ··   1857-1865,   "   .5
Special   "   "   ··   1866-1870,   "   6
   "   "   "   ··   1871-1875,   "   7
   "   "   "   "   1876-1880,   "   8
   "   "   "   "   1881-1884,   "   9
   "   "   "   ··   1885-1889,   "   10
   "   "   "   "   1893,   "   11
   "   "   "   ··   1895 & 1897,   "   12
   "   "   "   "   1899 & 1901,   "   13
   "   "   .."   "   1903.
Statutes of Connecticut, ...   1838
   "   "   "   1854
General Statutes of Connecticut, Revision of   1866
   "   "   "   "   "   "   1875
   "   "   and Public Acts of Connecticut, 1875-1882
   "   "   of Connecticut,   .   .   .   1888
   "   "   "   "   Revision of   1902

REPORTS OF ATTORNEY-GENERALS.

Report	of	Attorney-General	of	Alabama,	1898, 1900
"	"	"	"	"	1900
"	"	"	"	California,	1895-1896, 1899-1900
			"	"	1899-1900
			"	Colorado,	1897-1898
			"	"	1899-1900
			"	Georgia,	1896, 1898, 1900, 1902
			"	"	1897
			"	"	1898
			"	"	1900
			"	Idaho,	1901-1902
			"	Indiana,	1895-1896
			"	"	1897-1898
			"	"	1899-1900
			"	Illinois,	1897-1898-1901-1902
			"	"	1897-1898
			"	Iowa,	1897, 1898, 1899,-1902-'03
			"	"	1898
			"	"	1899
			"	Kansas,	1895-'96-'97-'98-'99-'00-'01-'02
			"	"	1897-1898
"	"	•	"	"	1899-1900
			"	Louisiana,	1898
			"	Maine,	1893-1894-1897-1898
			"	"	1897-1898
			"	Massachusetts,	189
			"	Michigan,	1897, 1898, 1899, 1901, '02
..	..	.	..	"	1898
				"	1899
					1901
			"	"	1902
			"	Minnesota,	1894, 1896, 1902
			"	"	1896
			"	Mississippi,	1901-1903
		••	. "	Montana,	1897-1898
			"	"	1899-1900
			"	Nebraska,	1897-1898, 1902
			"	New York, 1889, '91, '95, '96, '97, '98	
			"	"	1891
			"	"	1895
					1896
					1897
			"	"	1898
			"	North Carolina, 1899-1900, 1901-1902	
			"	North Dakota,	1896
			"	Oregon,	1903-1904

MISCELLANEOUS.

INDEX TO ACTIONS WITHIN THE STATE.

INDEX TO ACTIONS OUTSIDE THE STATE.

INDEX TO OPINIONS.

CPSIA information can be obtained
at www.ICGtesting.com
Printed in the USA
BVHW04*1211180918
527831BV00013B/940/P